LEVEL H

VOCABULARY

word meaning, pronunciation, prefixes, suffixes, synonyms, antonyms, and fun!

in Action

LOYOLA PRESS.

Chicago

LOYOLA PRESS.

3441 N. Ashland Avenue
Chicago, Illinois 60657
(800) 621-1008
www.loyolapress.com

Cover & Interior Art: Anni Betts
Cover Design: Judine O'Shea
Interior Design: Kathy Greenholdt

Copyright © 2010 Loyola Press

Manufactured in the United States of America.

ISBN-10: 0-8294-2781-3
ISBN-13: 978-0-8294-2781-3

10 11 12 13 14 15 16 17 Hess 10 9 8 6 7 5 4 3 2 1

VISIT
www.vocabularyinaction.com
ACCESS CODE: **VTB-8994**

Contents

Pronunciation Key

This key shows the meanings of the abbreviations and symbols used throughout the book.

Some English words have more than one possible pronunciation. This book gives only one pronunciation per word, except when different pronunciations indicate different parts of speech. For example, when the word *relay* is used as a noun, it is pronounced rē´ lā; as a verb, the word is pronounced rə lā´.

Parts of Speech

adj.	adjective	*int.*	interjection	*prep.*	preposition
adv.	adverb	*n.*	noun	*part.*	participle
				v.	verb

Vowels

ā	tape	ə	about, circus	ôr	torn
a	map	ī	kite	oi	noise
âr	stare	i	win	ou	foul
ä	car, father	ō	toe	ōo	soon
ē	meet	o	mop	ŏo	book
e	kept	ô	law	u	tug

Consonants

ch	check	ŋ	rang	y	yellow
g	girl	th	thimble	zh	treasure
j	jam	th	that	sh	shelf

Stress

The accent mark follows the syllable receiving the major stress, such as in the word *plaster* (plas´ tər).

Introduction

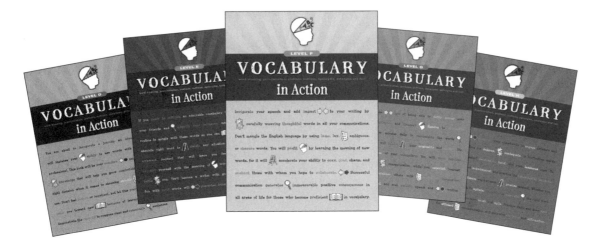

Vocabulary in Action is the premier vocabulary development program that increases students' literacy skills and improves test scores.

Researchers and educators agree that vocabulary development is essential in learning how to communicate effectively through listening, speaking, reading, and writing. The National Reading Panel (2000) has identified vocabulary as one of the five areas that increase students' reading ability. After the third grade, reading difficulties are often attributed to a vocabulary deficit—an inability to understand word meaning.

Vocabulary in Action offers the following elements to help students develop this critical literacy skill:

- Flexible leveling and student placement for individualized instruction

- Words that were researched and selected specifically for frequency, occurrence, and relevance to assessment and everyday life

- Intentional, direct instruction focused on words and their meanings, usage, and relationships to other words

- Repeated word appearance in a variety of contexts for extensive exposure and practice with literal and figurative meanings

- Application of new vocabulary skills through practice exercises, assessments, and standardized test preparation opportunities

Program Overview

Each Student Book includes

- **Program Pretest** to identify level of understanding

- **Research-based Word Lists** selected for frequency, occurrence, and relevance to assessment

- **One Hundred or More Related Words** including synonyms and antonyms

- **Word Pronunciations, Meanings, and Identifications of Parts of Speech**

- **At Least a Dozen Activities per Chapter,** including activities for words in context, word meaning, word usage, related words, and word building

- **Challenge Words and Activities**

- **Fun with Words** activities for additional practice

- **Test-Taking Tips** section covering test-taking skills, testing formats, and study of testing vocabulary including classic roots, prefixes, and suffixes

- **Special Features** for etymology, mnemonic devices, historical facts, word trivia, and word origin

- **Notable Quotes** that show words in context

- **Chapter Review Assessments** for multiple chapters

- **Program Posttest** to determine overall growth

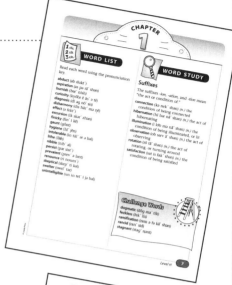

Total Vocabulary Word Count by Level

LEVEL	WORDS TO KNOW	ADDITIONAL WORDS
D	150	over 100
E	225	over 150
F, G, H	375	over 200

Each Teacher Guide includes

- **Annotated Guide** similar to the student book for easy correction

- **Additional Games and Activities** for a variety of groupings, learning styles, multiple intelligences, and levels of proficiency in English

- **Suggestions for Guided and Independent Practice**

- **Academic Language Practice** with games and activities, including work with classic roots

- **Icons** for easy identification

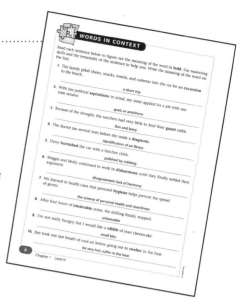

The *Vocabulary in Action* Web site includes

- Assessments

- Pretests and Reviews

- Word Lists and Definitions

- Vocabulary Games

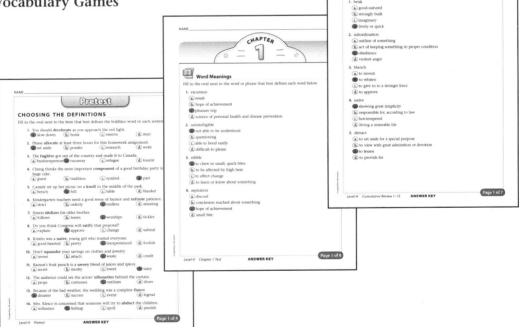

How to Implement This Program

With *Vocabulary in Action*, it is easy to differentiate instruction to meet the needs of all students.

Student Placement

Use the following chart to help determine the book most appropriate for each individual student. Differences in level include word difficulty, sentence complexity, and ideas presented in context. In addition to the chart, consider a student's achievement level on any pretest that you give. Adjust books based on a student's achievement on a pretest and other vocabulary assignments, his or her ability to retain new information, and the student's overall work ethic and interest level.

Placement Levels

Typical Grade-Level Assignments		Accelerated Grade-Level Assignments	
LEVEL	GRADE	LEVEL	GRADE
D	4	D	3
E	5	E	4
F	6	F	5
G	7	G	6
H	8	H	7

To Begin

At the beginning of the year, choose a book for each student based on the above criteria. Have each student take the program pretest in his or her book. Avoid timing the test. Give students enough time to complete the test thoughtfully and with confidence. After grading the test and noting student achievement levels, make book adjustments if necessary.

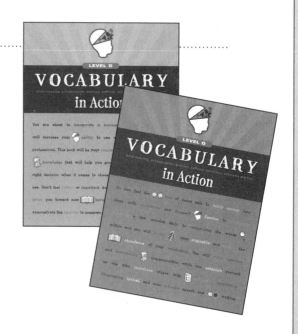

Work Through the Chapters

Follow these steps to implement each chapter.

1. **Chapter opener:** Have students work with partners, in small groups, or with you to read aloud each word in the **Word List.** Check pronunciation and discuss the definition of each word, having students find the words in a dictionary if you have time. Have students review the **Word Study** section. Introduce the **Challenge Words** in the same way as the Word List. Then have students remove the page and complete the back side.

2. **Chapter pages:** Based on students' confidence and ability, assign students to complete chapter activities independently, with you, with peers, or as homework. Students should complete activities for Words in Context, Word Meanings, Use Your Vocabulary, Word Learning, Synonyms, Antonyms, Word Study, Challenge Words, and Fun with Words. Provide support through modeling and discussion. Here are some approaches:

   • Teacher presents and completes a page with students during the first 10 or 15 minutes of each reading or language arts session. Pages are reviewed simultaneously as guided practice.

   • Students complete chapter pages in class after other reading or language arts assignments are complete. Pages are collected and reviewed after class.

   • Students complete chapter pages as homework assignments, one page per night. Pages are collected and reviewed after completion.

3. **Reteaching/additional practice:** Monitor student progress on a regular basis. If students need additional practice, use the **Games & Activities** on pages 189–194 of this guide or the **Teacher Activities** on pages 195–196.

4. **Standardized test preparation:** At least one month prior to standardized testing, work with students to complete pages 183–184.

5. **Chapter reviews:** After completing every three chapters, administer the Chapter Review to note students' progress and to identify difficult words.

6. **Assessment:** Have students complete a formal assessment after each chapter. Visit **www.vocabularyinaction.com** and access the assessment with this code: **VTB-8994.** You can also access a **Pretest** and **Review.**

Sample Yearly Plan for Level H

Following is one way to implement *Vocabulary in Action* for Level H.

WEEK	STUDENT BOOK	RELATED ACTIVITIES	
1	Pretest		
2–3	Chapter 1	Games & Activities (pp. 189–194) Teacher Activities (pp. 195–196)	Chapter 1 Assessment
4–5	Chapter 2	Games & Activities (pp. 189–194) Teacher Activities (pp. 195–196)	Chapter 2 Assessment
6–7	Chapter 3	Games & Activities (pp. 189–194) Teacher Activities (pp. 195–196)	Chapter 3 Assessment
8	Review Chapters 1–3	Online Games (www.vocabularyinaction.com) Cumulative Review	
9–10	Chapter 4	Games & Activities (pp. 189–194) Teacher Activities (pp. 195–196)	Chapter 4 Assessment
11–12	Chapter 5	Games & Activities (pp. 189–194) Teacher Activities (pp. 195–196)	Chapter 5 Assessment
13–14	Chapter 6	Games & Activities (pp. 189–194) Teacher Activities (pp. 195–196)	Chapter 6 Assessment
15	Review Chapters 4–6	Online Games (www.vocabularyinaction.com) Cumulative Review	
16–17	Chapter 7	Games & Activities (pp. 189–194) Teacher Activities (pp. 195–196)	Chapter 7 Assessment
18–19	Chapter 8	Games & Activities (pp. 189–194) Teacher Activities (pp. 195–196)	Chapter 8 Assessment
20–21	Chapter 9	Games & Activities (pp. 189–194) Teacher Activities (pp. 195–196)	Chapter 9 Assessment
22	Review Chapters 7–9	Online Games (www.vocabularyinaction.com) Cumulative Review	
23	Chapter 10	Games & Activities (pp. 189–194) Teacher Activities (pp. 195–196)	Chapter 10 Assessment
24–25	Chapter 11	Games & Activities (pp. 189–194) Teacher Activities (pp. 195–196)	Chapter 11 Assessment
26–27	Chapter 12	Games & Activities (pp. 189–194) Teacher Activities (pp. 195–196)	Chapter 12 Assessment
28	Review Chapters 10–12	Online Games (www.vocabularyinaction.com) Cumulative Review	
29	Chapter 13	Games & Activities (pp. 189–194) Teacher Activities (pp. 195–196)	Chapter 13 Assessment
30–31	Chapter 14	Games & Activities (pp. 189–194) Teacher Activities (pp. 195–196)	Chapter 14 Assessment
32–33	Chapter 15	Games & Activities (pp. 189–194) Teacher Activities (pp. 195–196)	Chapter 15 Assessment
34	Review Chapters 13–15	Online Games (www.vocabularyinaction.com) Cumulative Review	
35	Posttest		

Pretest

This test contains some of the words you will find in this book. It will give you an idea of the kinds of words you will study. When you have completed all the chapters, the Posttest will measure what you have learned.

CHOOSING THE DEFINITIONS

Fill in the bubble next to the item that best defines the boldface word in each sentence.

Ch. 1 **1.** The doctor's **diagnosis** was a relief to the whole family.
  ⓐ instruction 🅑 conclusion ⓒ medicine ⓓ conversation

Ch. 1 **2.** We feel and look better when we practice good **hygiene** every day.
  ⓐ house cleaning 🅑 promptness 🅒 personal health ⓓ honesty

Ch. 10 **3.** Noah was **despondent** when his best friend moved away.
  ⓐ elated 🅑 furious ⓒ solitary 🅓 depressed

Ch. 3 **4.** The citizens committee turned the **dilapidated** warehouse into a recreation center.
  ⓐ enormous 🅑 stone ⓒ abandoned 🅓 ruined

Ch. 2 **5.** The **glutton** at the banquet annoyed everyone.
  🅐 greedy eater 🅑 long table ⓒ main dish ⓓ staff of waiters

Ch. 12 **6.** An angry bear is a **ferocious** beast.
  🅐 savage 🅑 playful ⓒ strong ⓓ clumsy

Ch. 1 **7.** The desert is beautiful, but the afternoon sun may make us **swelter**.
  ⓐ search for water 🅑 get lost ⓒ seek shelter 🅓 suffer from heat

Ch. 2 **8.** My friend and I leave notes for each other in a shallow **niche** in the stone wall.
  🅐 cavern 🅑 hole ⓒ glass box ⓓ shelf

Ch. 1 **9.** Mom said the loud music from the stereo was **intolerable**.
  🅐 pleasant 🅑 unbearable ⓒ exciting ⓓ deafening

Ch. 4 **10.** His friend's request caused a serious **dilemma** for Andy.
  🅐 illness 🅑 expression 🅒 choice ⓓ crime

Ch. 4 **11.** You can spread happiness by performing **random** acts of kindness.
  ⓐ generous 🅑 unplanned ⓒ planned ⓓ silent

Ch. 8 **12.** **Famine** forced some immigrants to move to the United States.
  ⓐ government 🅑 persecution ⓒ injustice 🅓 starvation

Ch. 1 13. The blue gill is the most **prevalent** fish in Eagle Lake.
    a. freshwater   **b.** common   **c.** poisonous   **d.** rare

Ch. 5 14. Ever since that incident, Albert has held a **grudge** against Omar.
    a. resentment   **b.** kindness   **c.** sadness   **d.** indifference

Ch. 9 15. Her **affinity** for animals may lead her to become a veterinarian.
    a. dislike   **b.** ownership   **c.** fondness   **d.** fear

Ch. 3 16. Our class circulated a **petition** to keep the after-school program.
    a. chain letter   **b.** magazine   **c.** written request   **d.** survey

Ch. 2 17. Even though Kwan speaks Chinese, she has trouble understanding her new friend's **dialect**.
    a. conversation   **b.** pronunciation   **c.** idea   **d.** picture

Ch. 3 18. I like to sing, but I can never remember the **lyrics**.
    a. words   **b.** tunes   **c.** titles   **d.** keys

Ch. 5 19. I dislike the artist's style, but I admire her **diligence**.
    a. imagination   **b.** skill   **c.** hard work   **d.** collection

Ch. 2 20. After the power failure, we had to **synchronize** all our clocks.
    a. compare   **b.** wind   **c.** take apart   **d.** match times on

Ch. 10 21. Building a stone wall is a **laborious** task.
    a. difficult   **b.** long   **c.** simple   **d.** unionized

Ch. 4 22. Cal's neighborhood is full of friendly and **upright** citizens.
    a. well-known   **b.** morally good   **c.** uncaring   **d.** concerned

Ch. 4 23. The fans all **idolize** the team's quarterback.
    a. adore   **b.** mimic   **c.** fear   **d.** criticize

Ch. 7 24. **Disposal** of toxic materials is an important environmental issue.
    a. manufacturing   **b.** using   **c.** discarding   **d.** collection

Ch. 3 25. The senator's reaction to the scandal may **taint** his reputation.
    a. make fun of   **b.** describe   **c.** harm   **d.** praise

Ch. 5 26. Our science teacher showed us how to create a **vacuum** in a container.
    a. vapor   **b.** empty space   **c.** model   **d.** experiment

Ch. 3 27. Rescue workers rushed to the site of the **catastrophe**.
    a. festival   **b.** disaster   **c.** drill   **d.** convention

Ch. 5 28. The racers ran to the pole, **pivoted** around it, and hopped back.
    a. rotated   **b.** dug   **c.** danced   **d.** landscaped

Ch. 6 29. Dad tried to **dilute** the old paint with turpentine.
    a. mix   **b.** remove   **c.** apply   **d.** thin

Ch. 14 30. The jurors felt that the doctor was a **credible** witness.
    a. dramatic   **b.** unbelievable   **c.** reliable   **d.** medical

Ch. 6 31. The scientists prepared for the **venture** in the rainforest.
    a. risky task   **b.** village   **c.** camping trip   **d.** film crew

Ch. 6 32. The quiz show contestant made a **haphazard** guess.
    a. educated   **b.** chance   **c.** desperate   **d.** dangerous

Ch. 4 33. Sara didn't realize that her **flippant** remark would hurt Sandy's feelings.
    a. offhand   **b.** friendly   **c.** noisy   **d.** nasty

Ch. 6 34. The principal asked for volunteers to make a **platform** for the exhibit.
    a. advertisement   **b.** guidebook   **c.** raised floor   **d.** area

Ch. 7 35. The **dimensions** of the crate are large enough for the statue.
    a. contents   **b.** measurements   **c.** decorations   **d.** sides

Ch. 5 36. We like the food in the new restaurant, but the service is **mediocre**.
    a. magnificent   **b.** terrible   **c.** slow   **d.** ordinary

Ch. 7 37. After marching all day, the exhausted **platoon** returned to the base.
    a. animal   **b.** military group   **c.** commander   **d.** pirate

Ch. 8 38. Fred woke up early to begin his **hectic** day.
    a. very windy   **b.** ordinary   **c.** important   **d.** very hurried

Ch. 11 39. Bill and Paula are sure they can **engineer** a robot in time for the science fair.
    a. motorize   **b.** control   **c.** disassemble   **d.** build

Ch. 7 40. After the meal, the waiter brought out a tray of **savory** desserts.
    a. delicious   **b.** melting   **c.** bland   **d.** expensive

Ch. 8 41. Dorothy bought a **diminutive** curtain for the dollhouse.
    a. antique   **b.** torn   **c.** tiny   **d.** lacy

Ch. 6 42. Anything that helps the environment is **beneficial** for everyone.
    a. popular   **b.** dangerous   **c.** helpful   **d.** harmful

Ch. 8 43. There must be a **plausible** explanation for the scary noise.
    a. unbelievable   **b.** believable   **c.** lengthy   **d.** confused

Ch. 15 44. The **perimeter** of the lake measures exactly three miles.
 a. depth **b.** distance around **c.** distance across **d.** width

Ch. 7 45. Even mountain climbers couldn't get up the **vertical** cliff.
 a. rocky **b.** sloping **c.** extremely high **d.** straight up and down

Ch. 9 46. We listened as the alleged felon tried to **hedge** the reporter's question.
 a. answer **b.** avoid **c.** ask **d.** shout

Ch. 8 47. The archaeologists found only a **vestige** of the ancient city.
 a. trace **b.** map **c.** exploration **d.** legend

Ch. 14 48. The engineers **devised** a plan to reroute traffic around the construction site.
 a. demolished **b.** opened **c.** revealed **d.** invented

Ch. 14 49. Grandpa spun a good **yarn** about his trip to Florida.
 a. joke **b.** nature essay **c.** adventure story **d.** travelogue

Ch. 9 50. No one has ever been able to discover the pirate's **plunder**.
 a. secret **b.** name **c.** good news **d.** stolen goods

Ch. 5 51. The baby penguin will **flourish** on the new diet.
 a. chew **b.** thrive **c.** get sick **d.** become overweight

Ch. 9 52. The **voluble** child wore out the babysitter.
 a. active **b.** obedient **c.** talkative **d.** moody

Ch. 10 53. When questioned by the police, the witness gave a **hesitant** answer.
 a. undecided **b.** incorrect **c.** firm **d.** positive

Ch. 8 54. The principal **commended** Alan's essay about the community.
 a. disliked **b.** praised **c.** read aloud **d.** graded

Ch. 10 55. Franco hoped for the opportunity to **portray** the detective.
 a. act the part of **b.** call for **c.** hire **d.** deceive

Ch. 11 56. Be firm but gentle when you **discipline** your new puppy.
 a. chase **b.** feed **c.** punish **d.** spoil

Ch. 2 57. The astronomer explained his **hypothesis** about asteroids.
 a. book **b.** understanding **c.** telescope **d.** theory

Ch. 10 58. The executives met to **transact** the business of joining the two companies.
 a. put an end to **b.** encourage **c.** carry out **d.** witness

Ch. 11 59. Grandma keeps a **hoard** of jelly beans for our visits.
a. stored supply b. large amount c. gift d. locked cabinet

Ch. 10 60. We all complained about the new manager's **dominant** personality.
a. largest b. obedient c. quietest d. controlling

Ch. 11 61. The **weary** traveler was glad when the long flight ended.
a. elderly b. tired c. experienced d. excited

Ch. 12 62. After moving to her new neighborhood, Kara felt **disconnected** from everyone.
a. sleepy b. pensive c. detached d. negative

Ch. 6 63. Mrs. Wells is my father's **colleague**.
a. partner b. enemy c. friend d. boss

Ch. 12 64. The new soldiers wondered if they would see the general's **wrath**.
a. rage b. plan c. flowers d. grief

Ch. 12 65. My brother was sent on a two-week **furlough**.
a. mission b. convention c. isolation d. vacation

Ch. 15 66. We planned to get an early start, but fate **intervened**.
a. interviewed b. helped out c. interfered d. questioned

Ch. 12 67. The scientist gave us a **precise** answer.
a. blurted b. exact c. incorrect d. garbled

Ch. 13 68. The stray kitten looked wet and **wretched**.
a. angry b. feverish c. striped d. miserable

Ch. 13 69. The rivalry between the teams caused **discord** between the two schools.
a. disagreement b. hysteria c. friendship d. good behavior

Ch. 13 70. The little mouse skillfully avoided the **predator**.
a. soldier b. trap c. hunter d. automobile

Ch. 12 71. Making a speech is an **ordeal** for Dan.
a. honor b. trial c. joy d. experience

Ch. 14 72. The **humble** firefighters declared that they were only doing their job.
a. quiet b. brilliant c. clumsy d. modest

Ch. 14 73. The drama coach held a **preliminary** meeting for everyone who wanted to try out for the play.
a. introductory b. informal c. long d. scheduled

Ch. 3 74. The flashbulb's bright light made the students **flinch**.
a. smile b. wince c. laugh d. sob

© Loyola Press.

Ch. 13 75. The chimp's show of **hostility** is only a game.
- a. good manners
- b. grief
- **c. unfriendliness**
- d. cheerfulness

Ch. 15 76. Rachel's mother helped her **disentangle** the ribbon from her hair.
- a. examine
- b. break
- c. tie
- **d. free**

Ch. 4 77. Kevin tried to act **nonchalant** about winning the race.
- a. smug
- b. excited
- c. unhappy
- **d. casual**

Ch. 15 78. The **presumptuous** journalist asked personal questions.
- **a. overconfident**
- b. accurate
- c. curious
- d. prompt

Ch. 15 79. The volunteer's **zeal** for the project made her its best worker.
- a. liveliness
- **b. enthusiasm**
- c. assignment
- d. donation

Ch. 1 80. When Aladdin **burnished** the lamp, the genie appeared.
- a. destroyed
- **b. polished**
- c. lit
- d. turned off

Ch. 11 81. Allie felt that boots would be the most **pragmatic** choice.
- a. difficult
- b. impractical
- c. expensive
- **d. practical**

Ch. 9 82. The talented **diplomat** brought an end to the crisis.
- a. chef
- b. graduate
- **c. ambassador**
- d. elected official

Ch. 9 83. The book store is small, but it has a **diverse** selection of books.
- a. large
- **b. varied**
- c. strange
- d. divided

Ch. 15 84. Flo leaped over the last **hurdle** to win the race.
- **a. barrier**
- b. player
- c. puddle
- d. shrub

Ch. 14 85. Abraham Lincoln is remembered as a **paragon** of honesty.
- a. story about
- **b. ideal example**
- c. mockery
- d. lacking

Ch. 13 86. The doctor's prescription was only **legible** to the druggist.
- a. unreadable
- b. legal
- c. written
- **d. clear**

Ch. 13 87. Bill felt a slight **twinge** when he ran on his sprained ankle.
- a. fall
- b. regret
- **c. pain**
- d. burn

Ch. 7 88. The pony **faltered** in front of the stream.
- **a. hesitated**
- b. jumped
- c. trotted
- d. drank

Ch. 2 89. The actor's **retort** made the audience cheer.
- **a. witty reply**
- b. training
- c. final exit
- d. sneer

Ch. 11 90. Later on, Luke came to **lament** his hasty remark.
- a. laugh at
- b. recall
- **c. regret**
- d. blame

Pretest   Level H

CHAPTER 1

WORD LIST

Read each word using the pronunciation key.

abduct (ab dukt´)
aspiration (as pə rā´ shən)
burnish (bər´ nish)
curiosity (kyŏŏr ē äs´ ə tē)
diagnosis (dī əg nō´ sis)
disharmony (dis här´ mə nē)
effect (ə fekt´)
excursion (ik skər´ zhən)
finicky (fin´ i kē)
gaunt (gônt)
hygiene (hī´ jēn)
intolerable (in täl´ ər ə bəl)
lithe (līth)
nibble (nib´ əl)
persist (pər sist´)
prevalent (prev´ ə lənt)
renounce (ri nouns´)
skeptical (skep´ ti kəl)
swelter (swel´ tər)
unintelligible (un in tel´ i jə bəl)

WORD STUDY

Suffixes

The suffixes *-ion*, *-ation*, and *-tion* mean "the act or condition of."

connection (kə nek´ shən) *(n.)* the condition of being connected
hibernation (hī bər nā´ shən) *(n.)* the act of hibernating
illumination (i lōō mə nā´ shən) *(n.)* the condition of being illuminated or lit
observation (ob sərv ā´ shən) *(n.)* the act of observing
rotation (rō tā´ shən) *(n.)* the act of rotating or turning around
satisfaction (sat is fak´ shən) *(n.)* the condition of being satisfied

Challenge Words

dogmatic (dôg ma´ tik)
feckless (fek´ lis)
ramification (ram ə fə kā´ shən)
rancid (ran´ sid)
stagnant (stag´ nənt)

■ **TEACHER TIP:** See page ix for suggestions on how to use this page.

WORDS IN CONTEXT

Read each sentence below to figure out the meaning of the word in **bold**. Use reasoning skills and the remainder of the sentence to help you. Write the meaning of the word on the line.

1. The family piled chairs, snacks, towels, and cameras into the car for an **excursion** to the beach.

   <u>a short trip</u>

2. With her political **aspirations** in mind, my sister applied for a job with our state senator.

   <u>goals or ambitions</u>

3. Because of the drought, the ranchers had very little to feed their **gaunt** cattle.

   <u>thin and bony</u>

4. The doctor ran several tests before she made a **diagnosis**.

   <u>identification of an illness</u>

5. Daisy **burnished** the car with a lint-free cloth.

   <u>polished by rubbing</u>

6. Maggie and Molly continued to work in **disharmony** until they finally settled their argument.

   <u>disagreement; lack of harmony</u>

7. We learned in health class that personal **hygiene** helps prevent the spread of germs.

   <u>the science of personal health and cleanliness</u>

8. After four hours of **intolerable** noise, the drilling finally stopped.

   <u>unbearable</u>

9. I'm not really hungry, but I would like a **nibble** of your cheesecake.

   <u>small bite</u>

10. Jim took one last breath of cool air before going out to **swelter** in the heat.

    <u>be very hot; suffer in the heat</u>

WORD MEANINGS

Word Learning

Study the spelling, part(s) of speech, and meaning(s) of each word. Complete each sentence by writing the word on the line. Then read the sentence.

1. **abduct** *(v.)* to carry off by force

   The villains intend to _____abduct_____ the millionaire's child.

2. **aspiration** *(n.)* a hope of achievement

   Since James's _____aspiration_____ is to become a musician, he practices the cello every day.

3. **burnish** *(v.)* 1. to polish by rubbing; 2. to make glossy and smooth

   My mother uses a special cream to _____burnish_____ the silver.

4. **curiosity** *(n.)* a desire to learn or know about something

   My _____curiosity_____ got the better of me, and I read the end of the book first.

5. **diagnosis** *(n.)* 1. an act of identifying a certain illness; 2. a conclusion reached about something

   After the test, we waited eagerly for the doctor's _____diagnosis_____.

6. **disharmony** *(n.)* 1. lack of agreement or harmony; 2. discord

   The barnyard animals mooed, honked, bleated, and crowed in _____disharmony_____.

7. **effect** *(n.)* 1. a result; 2. outcome caused by something; *(v.)* to bring about or cause to happen

   You do not understand the _____effect_____ of your actions.

   The president began to _____effect_____ changes in club procedures.

8. **excursion** *(n.)* 1. a short journey; 2. a pleasure trip

   Mr. Cruz wants to join our _____excursion_____ to the Museum of Medicine.

9. **finicky** *(adj.)* 1. difficult to please; 2. very fussy; 3. fastidious

   My sister is such a _____finicky_____ eater.

10. **gaunt** *(adj.)* 1. thin and bony; 2. angular

    Her wedding ring hung loosely on her _____gaunt_____ finger.

11. **hygiene** *(n.)* the science of personal health and disease prevention

    Be sure to practice good _____hygiene_____.

12. **intolerable** *(adj.)* 1. unbearable; 2. beyond what is acceptable

    Last summer we suffered _____intolerable_____ heat.

13. **lithe** *(adj.)* able to bend easily

    The _____lithe_____ gymnasts did somersaults across the mat.

14. **nibble** *(v.)* to eat or chew in small, quick bites; *(n.)* a small bite

    Watch that mouse _____nibble_____ at the peanut butter.

    I'll just have a _____nibble_____ of your sandwich.

15. **persist** *(v.)* 1. to refuse to stop; 2. to continue firmly in an action or a thought

    If you _____persist_____ in playing your music, I'll have to make a formal complaint.

16. **prevalent** *(adj.)* widely or commonly found

    The belief in independence is _____prevalent_____ among Americans.

17. **renounce** *(v.)* 1. to give up a title, a responsibility, or an activity; 2. to reject

    Many people _____renounce_____ their bad habits on New Year's Day.

18. **skeptical** *(adj.)* 1. doubting; 2. questioning; 3. not quickly or easily believing

    Kitty Jones claimed innocence, but the judge looked _____skeptical_____.

19. **swelter** *(v.)* to be affected by high heat

    We'll _____swelter_____ all day in the hot sun.

20. **unintelligible** *(adj.)* not able to be understood

    Nothing but _____unintelligible_____ noises came through the wall.

Notable Quotes

"Far away in the sunshine are my highest **aspirations**. I may not reach them, but I can look up and see their beauty, believe in them, and try to follow where they lead."

—Louisa May Alcott (1832–1888), novelist

Use Your Vocabulary

Choose the word from the Word List that best completes each sentence. Write the word on the line. You may use the plural form of nouns and the past tense of verbs if necessary.

When I heard that domesticated cats descended from the African wildcat, I was __1__, but then I read it in the encyclopedia. The information stirred my __2__, so I checked out several books about cats. Cheetahs were __3__ from their native habitats and were trained as hunting animals by royalty in the Middle East and India. The __4__ belief among experts is that today's Abyssinian cats probably look most like the cats that lived in ancient Egypt. The Sphynx cat is hairless and has large ears, so it looks __5__ even when healthy and well-fed. In 1851, the first cat show was held in England for people who had __6__ of greatness for their cats.

A cat has a(n) __7__ body that can twist and turn in amazing ways. It utters a variety of __8__ meows, hisses, yelps, and purrs, but a sensitive cat owner can tell the difference between expressions of hunger, anger, pain, and contentment. Also, a cat's owner may need to take a sick cat to see a veterinarian for a proper __9__ and medication. Many pets require grooming, but a cat looks after its own __10__ by licking its fur smooth and clean. A cat uses its long, rough tongue with the same __11__ as a hairbrush or a scrubbing brush. A cat does not have sweat glands, but it may pant when it begins to __12__ on a hot day. Cats have a coating at the back of their eyes. This coating reflects direct light like __13__ metal. A cat sets the boundaries of its territory and very rarely makes __14__ outside of that area. Several cats living in the same household may have their moments of __15__, but they usually learn to get along.

I have a very __16__ cat who eats only canned tuna. He eats only a few __17__ at a time. My mother finds it __18__ that he jumps onto the kitchen counter. "I will __19__ all responsibility for that cat if he does not stop!" she said. Fortunately, he has learned not to __20__.

1. _____ skeptical
2. _____ curiosity
3. _____ abducted
4. _____ prevalent
5. _____ gaunt
6. _____ aspirations
7. _____ lithe
8. _____ unintelligible
9. _____ diagnosis
10. _____ hygiene
11. _____ effect
12. _____ swelter
13. _____ burnished
14. _____ excursions
15. _____ disharmony
16. _____ finicky
17. _____ nibbles
18. _____ intolerable
19. _____ renounce
20. _____ persist

SYNONYMS

Synonyms are words that have the same or nearly the same meanings.

Part 1 Choose the word from the box that is the best synonym for each group of words. Write the word on the line.

aspiration	excursion	gaunt	hygiene
intolerable	lithe	prevalent	unintelligible

1. prominent, widespread, accepted _____ prevalent

2. cleanliness, sanitation, health _____ hygiene

3. a tour, jaunt, expedition _____ excursion

4. skinny, emaciated, scrawny, haggard _____ gaunt

5. unendurable, impossible _____ intolerable

6. ambition, yearning, desire _____ aspiration

7. flexible, supple, pliable _____ lithe

8. meaningless, incomprehensible _____ unintelligible

Part 2 Replace the underlined word with a word from the box that means the same or almost the same. Write your answer on the line.

persists	burnished	skeptical	diagnosis
swelter	abduct	renounce	

9. Uncle Jim offered his <u>analysis</u> of the situation by saying that we need more working space in the basement. _____ diagnosis

10. If the cold weather <u>lasts</u>, we will all go crazy. _____ persists

11. I have no wish to <u>sweat</u> in this heat until dinnertime. _____ swelter

12. The silver locket was <u>polished</u> by the blowing desert sand. _____ burnished

13. O my Queen! I beg of you, do not <u>forsake</u> your only daughter!
    _____ renounce

14. They tried to <u>kidnap</u> the senator but were caught. _____ abduct

15. The police remain <u>doubtful</u> about the thieves' intentions.

_____skeptical_____

 **ANTONYMS**

Antonyms are words that have opposite or nearly opposite meanings.

Part 1 Choose the word from the box that is the best antonym for each group of words. Write the word on the line.

burnish	disharmony	finicky	intolerable	skeptical

1. pleasing, satisfying, bearable _____intolerable_____

2. agreement, pleasant sounds _____disharmony_____

3. convinced, accepting, sure _____skeptical_____

4. not hard to please, easygoing _____finicky_____

5. dull, dim _____burnish_____

Part 2 Replace the underlined word with a word from the box that means the opposite or almost the opposite. Write your answer on the line.

unintelligible	renounce	gaunt	prevalent	lithe

6. Mrs. Lang stretched out her hands and looked at her <u>stiff</u> fingers.

_____lithe_____

7. In the dry grass, we saw a <u>stout</u> rabbit. _____gaunt_____

8. Such ideas are <u>rare</u> in this part of the country. _____prevalent_____

9. Ebenezer is unlikely to <u>keep</u> his vow. _____renounce_____

10. The cashier said something <u>meaningful</u>. _____unintelligible_____

WORD STUDY

Suffixes Choose the word from the box that best completes each sentence.

connection   hibernation   illumination

observation   rotation   satisfaction

1. Carey toasted the marshmallows to his _____satisfaction_____.

2. Woe to the hiker who disturbs the bear's winter _____hibernation_____.

3. After close _____observation_____, I grew to understand the ape's behavior.

4. Alex grew dizzy from watching the _____rotation_____ of the merry-go-round.

5. What is your _____connection_____ with the family?

6. The _____illumination_____ of the street lamps casts an eerie glow.

Vocabulary in Action

The words *effect* and *affect* are easy to confuse with each other. Even journalists and English teachers sometimes have to stop and think about whether their sentence calls for *effect* or *affect*.

The word *effect* is almost always a noun, while *affect* is almost always a verb. So you may find it helpful to determine whether the sentence needs a verb or a noun.

Examples of *affect*, a verb: We were deeply affected by the film. The weather affects our moods. The quality of your work affects your grades.

Examples of *effect*, a noun: The effect of the new rule on the children was profound. The effect of diligent study habits is better learning.

Here are three easy tips to help you determine which is the correct word in a sentence.

Tip 1: Determine whether the usage calls for a noun or a verb.

Tip 2: If a verb is needed, you will almost always choose "affect," which means "to change or alter."

Tip 3: When a noun is needed, you will almost always choose "effect," which means "a result."

CHALLENGE WORDS

Word Learning—Challenge!

Study the spelling, part of speech, and meaning(s) of each word. Complete each sentence by writing the word on the line. Then read the sentence.

1. **dogmatic** *(adj.)* 1. opinionated; 2. arrogant

    Her _____dogmatic_____ approach to the issue made it impossible to argue with her.

2. **feckless** *(adj.)* 1. ineffective; 2. irresponsible; 3. careless

    I hope you will not be influenced by Tom's _____feckless_____ behavior.

3. **ramification** *(n.)* 1. the result or outcome of an act; 2. a consequence

    Whoever pulled that prank obviously did not realize its _____ramification_____; we were cleaning up for hours.

4. **rancid** *(adj.)* 1. having an awful odor or taste; 2. offensive

    After being in the car all day, the meat had turned _____rancid_____.

5. **stagnant** *(adj.)* 1. stale; 2. not advancing or developing

    You won't catch any fish in that _____stagnant_____ pond.

Use Your Vocabulary—Challenge!

The Search Begins Checkerboard, your pet cat, has gotten out of the house and you haven't seen her in several days. You are worried that she can't take care of herself in the wild woods near your home. Using the Challenge Words above, write a story about your search for Checkerboard on a separate piece of paper. Be sure to include a beginning, a middle, and an end. Use your imagination to make the story interesting.

> *Notable Quotes*
>
> "Iron rusts from disuse; **stagnant** water loses its purity and in cold weather becomes frozen; even so does inaction sap the vigor of the mind."
>
> —Leonardo da Vinci (1452–1519), Italian inventor, artist, mathematician (from *The Notebooks*)

FUN WITH WORDS

Use the clues to complete the puzzle. Choose from the vocabulary words in this chapter.

Across

4. You have this when you set a goal.

6. This "killed" the cat that wanted to know too much.

7. You do this if you want something badly enough.

10. After you get one, you might want a second opinion.

11. Mice do this to cheese.

12. A ruler in trouble might _____ his throne or office.

13. A cause always has one.

Down

1. Always be _____ of a deal that sounds too good to be true.

2. Speech sounds like this on a bad phone connection.

3. If something is dull, you do this to it.

4. A radio broadcast in 1938 made people believe Martians were going to _____ them.

5. People who are this about food may cook for themselves.

7. A(n) _____ opinion is one held by many people.

8. You need this kind of body to compete as an Olympic diver.

9. You'll start to do this if you stay in the sun too long.

 WORD LIST

 WORD STUDY

Read each word using the pronunciation key.

absurd (əb sərd´)
astound (ə stound´)
calamity (kə lam´ ə tē)
decelerate (dē sel´ ə rāt)
dialect (dī´ ə lekt)
dishonor (dis on´ ər)
efficient (i fish´ ənt)
exert (ig zərt´)
finite (fī´ nīt)
glutton (glut´ ən)
hypothesis (hī päth´ ə sis)
inundate (in´ ən dāt)
luminous (loo´ mə nəs)
niche (nich)
persuasive (pər swā´ siv)
prohibit (prō hib´ it)
retort (ri tôrt´)
snare (snâr)
synchronize (siŋ´ krə niz)
upheaval (up hē´ vəl)

Analogies

Analogies show relationships between pairs of words. Study the relationships between the pairs of words in the analogies below.

chick is to **hen** as **kitten** is to **cat**

napkin is to **lap** as **tablecloth** is to **table**

cage is to **parakeet** as **aquarium** is to **fish**

Challenge Words

admonish (ad mon´ ish)
exacerbate (ig zas´ ər bāt)
expedient (ek spē´ dē ənt)
superfluous (soo pər´ floo əs)
versatile (vər´ sə təl)

Level H

■ **TEACHER TIP:** See page ix for suggestions on how to use this page.

WORDS IN CONTEXT

Read each sentence below to figure out the meaning of the word in **bold**. Use reasoning skills and the remainder of the sentence to help you. Write the meaning of the word on the line.

1. Although we had prepared for the hurricane, the effects of the **calamity** overwhelmed us.

   horrible event; catastrophe

2. When Nikki shouted a question from the audience, the comedian responded with a clever **retort**.

   a fast or witty response

3. With our grandfather's fishing net, Mark set a **snare** for the next person to walk through the door.

   trap

4. I **astounded** my friends with my new magic tricks.

   amaze or surprise

5. I made a **glutton** of myself at Thanksgiving dinner, and I paid for it in stomach pains.

   someone who eats too much

6. There is no **dishonor** in losing if you have performed well.

   a shame or disgrace; loss of honor

7. To calm my anger, I lifted my eyes to the **luminous**, starry sky.

   bright or well-lit

8. **Dialects** vary from region to region, and people in the South speak differently from people in the North.

   a special form of a language

9. Your ideas are **absurd**; I don't even want to hear them.

   foolish; unreasonable

10. If we **synchronize** our schedules, we'll be able to eat lunch together.

    coordinate; to make agree in time

WORD MEANINGS

Word Learning

Study the spelling, part(s) of speech, and meaning(s) of each word. Complete each sentence by writing the word on the line. Then read the sentence.

1. **absurd** *(adj.)* 1. ridiculous or unreasonable; 2. not true

   Please don't give me such _____**absurd**_____ requests on short notice.

2. **astound** *(v.)* 1. to fill with wonder; 2. to surprise

   Her marvelous talents continue to _____**astound**_____ me.

3. **calamity** *(n.)* 1. a disaster; 2. great distress or misfortune

   We managed to avoid a _____**calamity**_____ by putting out the fire right away.

4. **decelerate** *(v.)* to decrease the speed of

   Remember to _____**decelerate**_____ the car before pulling into the driveway.

5. **dialect** *(n.)* a variation of pronunciation, grammar, or vocabulary by a group within a language or region

   That man's _____**dialect**_____ is particular to a region in Mexico.

6. **dishonor** *(n.)* 1. loss of one's good name; 2. shame; *(v.)* 1. to deprive of one's good name; 2. to shame; 3. to disgrace

   The traitor's behavior was a great _____**dishonor**_____ to her country.

   Do not _____**dishonor**_____ my family by speaking to me that way!

7. **efficient** *(adj.)* operating well, without wasted time, energy, or material

   I see you've developed a very _____**efficient**_____ system of making shoes.

8. **exert** *(v.)* 1. to put into action; 2. to exercise or use

   Daniel had to _____**exert**_____ all of his strength to reach the top of the tree.

9. **finite** *(adj.)* 1. having an end; 2. having bounds or limits; 3. measurable

   The Earth has _____**finite**_____ reserves of oil.

10. **glutton** *(n.)* a person or an animal that eats too much

    "The _____**glutton**_____ didn't leave any spinach for me!" she said laughingly.

11. **hypothesis** *(n.)* an unproved theory, statement, or guess that is based on facts

    I'd like to test that _____**hypothesis**_____.

12. **inundate** (*v.*) 1. to overwhelm; 2. to overflow

The prize giveaway caused listeners to _____inundate_____ the radio station with phone calls.

13. **luminous** (*adj.*) 1. giving light; 2. full of light; 3. bright

A _____luminous_____ candle burned in the window.

14. **niche** (*n.*) 1. a hollow space within a wall, rock, or hill; 2. a place or position well-suited to the person in it

Marietta found her _____niche_____ playing the triangle in the school orchestra.

15. **persuasive** (*adj.*) having the ability to convince

She made a very _____persuasive_____ argument for donating the money.

16. **prohibit** (*v.*) to forbid an action by rule or law

The managers decided to _____prohibit_____ smoking in the restaurant.

17. **retort** (*v.*) 1. to answer quickly; 2. to reply with a prompt argument; (*n.*) a fast or witty response

After the accusation, the judge will expect you to _____retort_____.

My sister always has a quick _____retort_____ for any remark.

18. **snare** (*n.*) 1. a trap, usually with a noose, for catching animals; 2. any trap; (*v.*) to trap

The rangers set a _____snare_____ in the forest.

The villain prepared to _____snare_____ her victim.

19. **synchronize** (*v.*) 1. to make agree in time; 2. to match the rate of movement of two things

It's time to _____synchronize_____ our watches.

20. **upheaval** (*n.*) 1. the act of being thrown upward; 2. an uprising or a violent upset

The earthquake created a huge _____upheaval_____ of land.

> ## Notable Quotes
>
> "In the highest civilization, the book is still the highest delight. He who has once known its satisfactions is provided with a resource against **calamity**."
>
> —Ralph Waldo Emerson (1803–1882), poet, philosopher (from *Letters and Social Aims: Quotation and Originality*)

Use Your Vocabulary

Choose the word from the Word List that best completes each sentence. Write the word on the line. You may use the plural form of nouns and the past tense of verbs if necessary.

I was in the yard at my grandparents farm when the **1** struck. The sky had an eerie, **2** quality, although the clouds were quite dark. My grandparents listened to the tornado warnings on the radio. The radio announcer spoke with a heavy **3** that I couldn't understand. It had been raining all day. The fields and garden were **4** with water, but now the rain had stopped. The wind had **5** too. Everything was calm and still. Suddenly, my grandparents came out of the house, walking quickly with almost **6** steps. Grandma was carrying Larry, her plump, hefty cat.

"Head for the storm cellar," Grandpa said. "The tornado is headed right for us, and we have only a(n) **7** amount of time to get ready."

"I don't see any funnel cloud," I said. "Maybe the weather forecaster's **8** is wrong."

"Do you want to wait up here and find out?" Grandpa **9** . I looked again at the dark, swirling clouds and realized I was being **10** . There was no **11** in being prepared for the worst.

We headed for the storm cellar. Since Grandpa keeps the doors well-oiled, he did not have to **12** much effort to open them. Grandma keeps the cellar supplied and organized in a very **13** manner.

"I knew our furry, little **14** wouldn't be happy without his food," Grandma said with a grin. Larry jumped from Grandma's arms and settled into a(n) **15** at the back of the cellar.

Without warning, the roar of the tornado filled the cellar and **16** conversation. I was **17** by the way the locked doors shook and rattled. Even Grandpa's hunting **18** , hanging under the stairs, swayed back and forth.

We were lucky. The **19** of several big trees on the property only damaged some fences. Seeing the areas directly hit by the tornado was a(n) **20** lesson. I'll take tornado warnings seriously from now on.

1. _____ calamity
2. _____ luminous
3. _____ dialect
4. _____ inundated
5. _____ decelerated
6. _____ synchronized
7. _____ finite
8. _____ hypothesis
9. _____ retorted
10. _____ absurd
11. _____ dishonor
12. _____ exert
13. _____ efficient
14. _____ glutton
15. _____ niche
16. _____ prohibited
17. _____ astounded
18. _____ snares
19. _____ upheaval
20. _____ persuasive

SYNONYMS

Synonyms are words that have the same or nearly the same meanings.

Part 1 Choose the word from the box that is the best synonym for each group of words. Write the word on the line.

astound	decelerate	finite	hypothesis
persuasive	retort	snare	upheaval

1. eruption, agitation, unrest   _____upheaval_____

2. effective, convincing, influential   _____persuasive_____

3. opinion, theory, supposition   _____hypothesis_____

4. respond; quick answer   _____retort_____

5. restricted, limited, bounded   _____finite_____

6. slow down   _____decelerate_____

7. amaze, shock, bewilder   _____astound_____

8. net, lure; entangle   _____snare_____

Part 2 Replace the underlined word with a word from the box that means the same or almost the same. Write your answer on the line.

luminous	inundated	exert	calamity
niche	absurd	prohibit	

9. The new laws will <u>prevent</u> parking on the streets at night. _____prohibit_____

10. The baby bird sat tucked in a <u>cranny</u> in the wall. _____niche_____

11. From miles away, we could see the <u>glowing</u> city lights. _____luminous_____

12. The catalog was <u>flooded</u> with orders for new computers. _____inundated_____

13. After his surgery, my father was not allowed to <u>strain</u> himself.
_____exert_____

14. It took the family months to recover from the <u>disaster</u>. _____calamity_____

15. Who would be so <u>foolish</u> as to eat peas with a knife? _____absurd_____

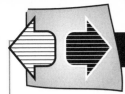

ANTONYMS

Antonyms are words that have opposite or nearly opposite meanings.

Part 1 Choose the word from the box that is the best antonym for each group of words. Write the word on the line.

decelerate	absurd	persuasive	snare	hypothesis

1. rational, reasonable, logical _____absurd_____

2. speed up, accelerate _____decelerate_____

3. free, let go, liberate _____snare_____

4. proven fact _____hypothesis_____

5. discouraging, deterring _____persuasive_____

Part 2 Replace the underlined word with a word from the box that means the opposite or almost the opposite. Write your answer on the line.

prohibit	upheaval	luminous	efficient	finite

6. The winter was a time of great <u>stillness</u> in our house. _____upheaval_____

7. The children had a <u>limitless</u> supply of toys. _____finite_____

8. Our heating system is very <u>wasteful</u>. _____efficient_____

9. Every house on the block had <u>dark</u> windows. _____luminous_____

10. Our neighbors did not want to <u>permit</u> snowball throwing in the street.
_____prohibit_____

Vocabulary in Action

The word **luminous** ("full of light") first appeared around 1432 and comes from the Latin word *luminosus*, which means "shining, full of light." Other words with the same Latin root include *translucent* and *illuminate*.

Analogies To complete the following analogies, decide what kind of relationship is shown by the first pair of words. Then fill in the bubble next to the pair of words that show the same relationship.

1. **hinder** is to **help** as
   - (a.) spray is to dig
   - (b.) forbid is to permit
   - (c.) think is to consider
   - (d.) scrape is to cut

2. **irritate** is to **mosquito** as
   - (a.) climb is to bumblebee
   - (b.) befriend is to spider
   - (c.) entertain is to comedian
   - (d.) sell is to lawyer

3. **scamper** is to **squirrel** as
   - (a.) glide is to airplane
   - (b.) rest is to nest
   - (c.) joke is to clown
   - (d.) eat is to chipmunk

4. **native** is to **foreign** as
   - (a.) friendly is to talkative
   - (b.) funny is to laughable
   - (c.) adventurous is to wonderful
   - (d.) familiar is to unknown

5. **compose** is to **poem** as
   - (a.) study is to library
   - (b.) write is to idea
   - (c.) construct is to house
   - (d.) earn is to bank

6. **depart** is to **farewell** as
   - (a.) arrive is to greeting
   - (b.) forget is to congratulation
   - (c.) sail is to departure
   - (d.) arrive is to expectation

Vocabulary in Action

To better understand analogies, rephrase the analogy in words that explain the relationships between the objects in the analogy. For example, in the analogy "chick is to hen as kitten is to cat," you might write "This analogy gives examples of baby animals and their adult counterparts." For the analogy "napkin is to lap as tablecloth is to table," you might say "The first items in each series cover and protect the second items in the analogy." How might you rephrase or describe the third analogy in the Word Study?

CHALLENGE WORDS

Word Learning—Challenge!

Study the spelling, part of speech, and meaning(s) of each word. Complete each sentence by writing the word on the line. Then read the sentence.

1. **admonish** *(v.)* to criticize or scold someone in a mild way

   Melissa _____admonished_____ her younger brother for teasing the chipmunk.

2. **exacerbate** *(v.)* 1. to make something worse than it is; 2. to aggravate

   If you also come late you will only _____exacerbate_____ the situation.

3. **expedient** *(adj.)* 1. useful for creating a desired result; 2. based on self-interest

   It would be most _____expedient_____ to park the car right in front.

4. **superfluous** *(adj.)* in excess of what is called for or necessary

   I have no need for this _____superfluous_____ chatter.

5. **versatile** *(adj.)* 1. able to do a number of things right; 2. useful for many functions

   I am looking for a _____versatile_____ jacket for both winter and spring.

Use Your Vocabulary—Challenge!

Project Protect After a tornado hit their town, all of the town's schools decide to build tornado shelters. They don't want to be caught unprepared by the next tornado. Jackie and Sam are in charge of organizing the shelter for their school, but they don't always get along with each other. Using the Challenge Words above, write a story about their project. Explain the problems they face and the solutions they reach.

Notable Quotes

"Animation can explain whatever the mind of man can conceive. This facility makes it the most **versatile** and explicit means of communication yet devised for quick mass appreciation."

—Walt Disney (1901–1966), film producer and pioneer of animated cartoon films

FUN WITH WORDS

Create a word search using 10 vocabulary words from the Basic Words list. Trade with a friend. Who can finish the word search first?

Answers will vary.

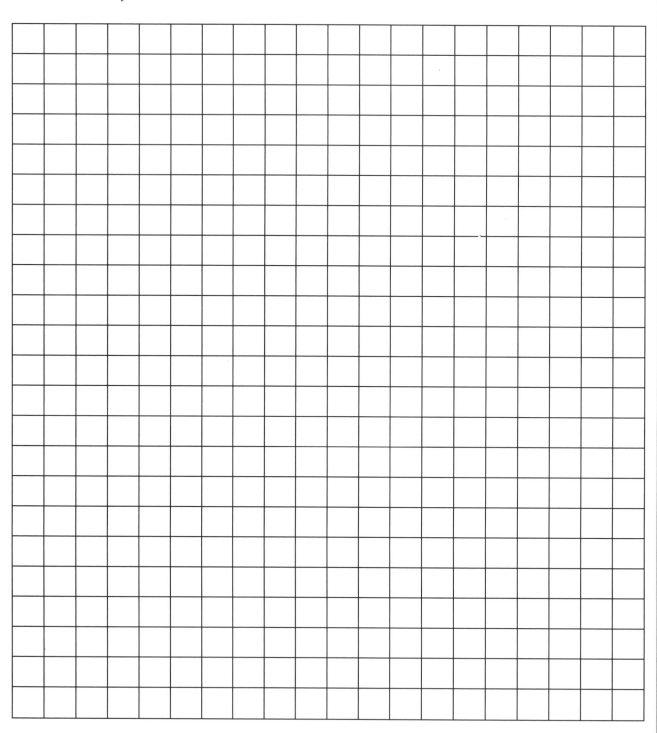

CHAPTER 3

WORD LIST

Read each word using the pronunciation key.

accessory (ak ses´ ə rē)
avenge (ə venj´)
catastrophe (kə tas´ trə fē)
decompose (dē kəm pōz´)
dilapidated (di lap´ ə dāt id)
dismay (dis mā´)
elapse (i laps´)
exhaust (ig zôst´)
flinch (flinch)
gorge (gôrj)
hysteria (his târ´ ē ə)
irascible (i ras´ ə bəl)
lyrics (lēr´ iks)
nominee (näm ə nē´)
petition (pə tish´ ən)
quirk (kwərk)
ruckus (ruk´ əs)
sopping (säp´ piŋ)
taint (tānt)
upkeep (up´ kēp)

WORD STUDY

Root Words

The Latin root *ag* or *act* means "to do" or "to drive."

action (ak´ shən) *(n.)* the state of doing something
active (ak´ tiv) *(n.)* tending to action; busy
agenda (ə jen´ də) *(n.)* a list of things to be done
agent (ā´ jənt) *(n.)* someone who does something
agile (aj´ əl) *(adj.)* able to do or move easily and quickly
enact (en akt´) *(v.)* to cause to be done

Challenge Words

anomaly (ə näm´ ə lē)
lucid (lo͞o´ sid)
misconstrue (mis cun stro͞o´)
mundane (mun dān´)
reprieve (ri prēv´)

■ **TEACHER TIP:** See page ix for suggestions on how to use this page.

WORDS IN CONTEXT

Read each sentence below to figure out the meaning of the word in **bold**. Use reasoning skills and the remainder of the sentence to help you. Write the meaning of the word on the line.

1. I don't understand the meaning of the **lyrics** to that song.

words to a song

2. Each political party will choose a presidential **nominee** at its convention.

person chosen as a candidate

3. Spring rains on the plateau caused flash flooding in the **gorge**.

small canyon or passage between mountains

4. Please stop that **ruckus**, or you'll wake the baby!

loud noise or disturbance

5. We felt **dismay** after seeing all the litter at the campsite.

discouraged or troubled

6. The countess planned to **avenge** the wrongs done to her father.

get revenge for

7. I have been in charge of the **upkeep** of my room since I was six years old.

maintenance; the act of keeping something in good condition

8. The roof of that **dilapidated** old cottage is about to cave in.

falling down or in bad condition

9. An hour **elapsed** while we waited for Ramona to come home.

passed

10. My stepfather thinks that if I tell too many jokes in class, it will **taint** my reputation as a serious student.

dirty; make less pure

WORD MEANINGS

Word Learning

Study the spelling, part(s) of speech, and meaning(s) of each word. Complete each sentence by writing the word on the line. Then read the sentence.

1. **accessory** *(n.)* 1. an extra element or feature; 2. one who helps in a crime

   My cousin said the sun roof was an _____accessory_____ she definitely wanted on her car.

2. **avenge** *(v.)* 1. to return some wrongdoing; 2. to take revenge

   Callie swore she would _____avenge_____ the hurtful insult.

3. **catastrophe** *(n.)* a great, sudden disaster

   The accident proved to be a life-threatening _____catastrophe_____.

4. **decompose** *(v.)* 1. to break down into parts; 2. to decay

   Dead plants and animals eventually _____decompose_____ on the forest floor.

5. **dilapidated** *(adj.)* 1. in a state of ruin or disrepair; 2. falling to pieces

   He kept his paintings in a _____dilapidated_____ barn.

6. **dismay** *(v.)* 1. to fill with fear; 2. to discourage or trouble; *(n.)* 1. fear at danger or trouble; 2. troubled state of mind

   Don't let my snake _____dismay_____ you; it doesn't bite.

   Suong cast a look of _____dismay_____ at the unkempt garden.

7. **elapse** *(v.)* 1. to pass by; 2. to slip away, usually with regard to time

   Time will _____elapse_____ slowly when you have nothing to do.

8. **exhaust** *(v.)* 1. to use up; 2. to drain; 3. to let out air or fumes; *(n.)* fumes or gases from an engine

   If we keep eating, we will _____exhaust_____ our supply of snacks.

   The bus let out a thick black _____exhaust_____.

9. **flinch** *(v.)* 1. to show pain, fear, or surprise with a sudden movement; 2. to draw away

   I saw him _____flinch_____ as the door slammed.

10. **gorge** *(n.)* a deep, narrow passage with steep, rocky walls; *(v.)* to stuff with something

    Our donkeys could not cross the _____gorge_____.

    Don't _____gorge_____ yourself with Halloween candy.

11. **hysteria** *(n.)* uncontrollable fear or emotion

    The appearance of the flying saucer led to mass _____hysteria_____.

12. **irascible** *(adj.)* 1. quick to anger; 2. hot-tempered

    I had heard about the _____irascible_____ toddler, but I was not prepared for her tantrums.

13. **lyrics** *(n.)* the words of a song

    I like that melody, but I don't care for the _____lyrics_____.

14. **nominee** *(n.)* 1. a person who is nominated; 2. a person who is chosen as a political candidate

    The judges decided which _____nominee_____ would win the grand prize.

15. **petition** *(n.)* 1. a written request for a certain action; 2. a strong request; *(v.)* 1. to make a request; 2. to seek

    We will circulate a _____petition_____ to build a new school.

    The neighborhood committee will _____petition_____ the city council for better garbage removal.

16. **quirk** *(n.)* 1. an odd behavior or mannerism; 2. accident

    Through some _____quirk_____, Toni never paid for her ticket.

17. **ruckus** *(n.)* 1. a noisy commotion or disturbance; 2. an uproar

    Those construction workers cause such a _____ruckus_____!

18. **sopping** *(adj.)* soaking wet or drenched

    I came in from the rain with _____sopping_____ shoes.

19. **taint** *(n.)* 1. to stain the honor of; 2. to dirty

    This mistake will certainly _____taint_____ his name as a good carpenter.

20. **upkeep** *(n.)* the act of keeping something in proper condition

    My teacher has charged me with the _____upkeep_____ of the reading corner.

Use Your Vocabulary

Choose the word from the Word List that best completes each sentence. Write the word on the line. You may use the plural form of nouns and the past tense of verbs if necessary.

On October 8, 1871, __1__ struck the city of Chicago. The Great Chicago Fire killed hundreds of people and left thousands homeless. Chicago has no hills, mountains, or __2__ to stop the wind from spreading a fire. The firefighters did their best, but to their __3__, the blaze grew out of control in less than two hours. They __4__ as the flames jumped across the Chicago River and engulfed the downtown area. Some areas of the city were filled with __5__ wooden shacks; the fire roared through these areas and continued to grow.

__6__ swept through the city. People filled the streets. Hundreds waded into Lake Michigan to escape the blaze, hoping that their __7__ clothes would protect them. Before long, the fire had __8__ the fire department and most of its water supplies. Days __9__ before the fire was brought under control.

Some people believed that an arsonist and his __10__ started the fire, but no one was ever charged with the crime. According to another story, a(n) __11__ in Mrs. O'Leary's barn started the fire. The __12__ of a song about the fire claim that Mrs. O'Leary's cow started it by kicking over a lantern. Some __13__ citizens wanted to __14__ the damage by punishing the O'Learys. Eventually, it was decided that no one had set the fire on purpose; it had happened through some horrible __15__ of fate.

Even though much of the city had been destroyed, the citizens did not allow it to __16__. They did not want the losses from the fire to __17__ their reputation as a growing, bustling city. They began immediately to rebuild. The city government heard a(n) __18__ for a change in the construction of houses. Elected officials and __19__ helped pass a construction code that required new buildings in Chicago to be made of brick. To this day, the __20__ of buildings in Chicago requires strict adherence to the city's fire code.

1. _____catastrophe_____
2. _____gorges_____
3. _____dismay_____
4. _____flinched_____
5. _____dilapidated_____
6. _____Hysteria_____
7. _____sopping_____
8. _____exhausted_____
9. _____elapsed_____
10. _____accessory_____
11. _____ruckus_____
12. _____lyrics_____
13. _____irascible_____
14. _____avenge_____
15. _____quirk_____
16. _____decompose_____
17. _____taint_____
18. _____petition_____
19. _____nominees_____
20. _____upkeep_____

31

SYNONYMS

Synonyms are words that have the same or nearly the same meanings.

Part 1 Choose the word from the box that is the best synonym for each group of words. Write the word on the line.

hysteria	upkeep	quirk	dilapidated
catastrophe	sopping	petition	ruckus

1. maintenance, repair, preservation   upkeep

2. soaked, dripping, saturated   sopping

3. appeal, plea; ask, beg   petition

4. stir, fuss, hubbub   ruckus

5. consuming fear, panic, excitement   hysteria

6. irregularity, peculiarity, accident   quirk

7. run-down, neglected   dilapidated

8. a calamity, upheaval, destruction   catastrophe

Part 2 Replace the underlined word(s) with a word from the box that means the same or almost the same. Write your answer on the line.

decompose	avenge	taint	gorge
flinch	irascible	elapse	

9. My <u>crabby</u> neighbor does not like us to play ball in the yard.
   irascible

10. How much time will <u>pass</u> before the situation changes? _____ elapse

11. The garbage in the yard will soon <u>rot</u>. _____ decompose

12. I'm afraid those chemicals will <u>pollute</u> our drinking water. _____ taint

13. Let's <u>stuff</u> the sack with toys and candy. _____ gorge

14. She didn't even <u>wince</u> when the glass crashed to the floor. _____ flinch

15. He plotted to <u>get revenge</u> for the attack on his brother. _____ avenge

ANTONYMS

Antonyms are words that have opposite or nearly opposite meanings.

Part 1 Choose the word from the box that is the best antonym for each group of words. Write the word on the line.

decompose	dilapidated	gorge
irascible	sopping	taint

1. dry, dehydrated, arid _____sopping_____

2. calm, agreeable, gracious _____irascible_____

3. renewed, rebuilt, refinished _____dilapidated_____

4. empty; a mountain peak _____gorge_____

5. purify, cleanse _____taint_____

6. grow, improve _____decompose_____

Part 2 Replace the underlined word with a word from the box that means the opposite or almost the opposite. Write your answer on the line.

hysteria	avenge	petition	exhaust	dismayed

7. I will not <u>forgive</u> that betrayal. _____avenge_____

8. Don't <u>fill</u> our reserve of supplies for later. _____exhaust_____

9. She was <u>reassured</u> by the condition of her house after the storm. _____dismayed_____

10. Please submit a written <u>command</u> to the school board. _____petition_____

11. I was overcome with <u>calmness</u>. _____hysteria_____

WORD STUDY

Root Words Choose the word from the box that best completes each of the following sentences.

action	active	agenda
agent	agile	enact

1. Have you written the _____agenda_____ for this week's meeting?

2. Before I leave, I have to talk with my travel _____agent_____.

3. When are you going to clean your room? I'd like to see some _____action_____.

4. That girl has an _____active_____ membership in the outdoors club.

5. The village wants to _____enact_____ a law requiring everyone to recycle their trash.

6. My cat can't jump up on the counter anymore because she's not as _____agile_____ as she used to be.

Vocabulary in Action

It can be useful to study carefully a word's parts as a way of gaining a deeper understanding of the word. This is sometimes called parsing a word. When you parse a word, you give a grammatical description of the word and how it works in a sentence, or a part of speech. Using a good dictionary, see if you can parse some of the words below. Keep an eye out for surprising discoveries along the way!

Activism

Actionable

Agency

Agriculture

CHALLENGE WORDS

Word Learning—Challenge!

Study the spelling, part of speech, and meaning(s) of each word. Complete each sentence by writing the word on the line. Then read the sentence.

1. **anomaly** *(n.)* 1. something that is hard to classify; 2. something different

   Mei's exuberant nature makes her an _____ anomaly _____ in her quiet family.

2. **lucid** *(adj.)* 1. having full understanding; 2. clear

   Although Mrs. Cruz is 95 years old, she is still quite _____ lucid _____.

3. **misconstrue** *(adj.)* 1. to think of in an incorrect way; 2. to misunderstand

   Don't _____ misconstrue _____ his silence as anger.

4. **mundane** *(adj.)* everyday, ordinary, or commonplace

   The squirrel is a fairly _____ mundane _____ example of a wild animal.

5. **reprieve** *(v.)* to delay or temporarily relieve

   Robin Hood asked the king to _____ reprieve _____ his jail sentence.

Use Your Vocabulary—Challenge!

Diary Memories Mrs. O'Leary has left behind a diary with entries that describe her experiences during and after the Great Chicago Fire. Think about what you already know about Mrs. O'Leary. Imagine the experiences she might have had. Using the Challenge Words above, write a fictional diary entry. Use your imagination!

Vocabulary in Action

The word **mundane** comes from the Latin word *mundanus*, which means "belonging to the world." *Mundane* was originally designated as a way of distinguishing between that which was of the Church and that which was not of the Church. *Mundane* meant "worldly," "ordinary," or even "vulgar," as opposed to heavenly. Some synonyms for *mundane* include *dull, uninteresting, routine, everyday, commonplace, boring,* and *humdrum.*

FUN WITH WORDS

How closely did you read the story on page 35? Fill in the appropriate vocabulary word next to each clue. Then unscramble the circled letters to tell one theory about where the Great Chicago Fire started. Reread the story if you need help.

1. the words of a song

L (Y) R I C S

2. easily angered

(I) R A S C I (B) L E

3. a political appointee

(N) O M I N (E) E

4. to trouble or scare

D I S M (A) Y

5. to draw back suddenly

F (L) I N C H

6. a calamity

C A (T) A S T (R) O P H E

7. to stain

T (A) I N T

8. dripping wet

S (O) P P I (N) G

9. a ravine

G O (R) G (E)

10. car fumes

E X (H) A U (S) T

Answer:

I N   T H E   O ' L E A R Y ' S

B A R N

Review 1-3

Word Meanings Fill in the bubble next to the word that is best defined by each phrase.

1. to steal away
   - a. persist
   - **b. abduct**
   - c. astound
   - d. exert

2. a person who eats more than is healthy
   - **a. glutton**
   - b. nominee
   - c. curiosity
   - d. dialect

3. wringing wet
   - a. skeptical
   - b. prevalent
   - c. burnish
   - **d. sopping**

4. easily provoked or angered
   - a. finicky
   - **b. irascible**
   - c. intolerable
   - d. persuasive

5. to slow down
   - a. abduct
   - b. taint
   - c. inundate
   - **d. decelerate**

6. a state of disagreement
   - a. diagnosis
   - **b. disharmony**
   - c. dishonor
   - d. dismay

7. disease prevention through good health
   - a. petition
   - b. hypothesis
   - c. upheaval
   - **d. hygiene**

8. to be uncomfortably hot
   - a. decelerate
   - b. prohibit
   - **c. swelter**
   - d. exhaust

9. to get even for a wrongdoing
   - **a. avenge**
   - b. retort
   - c. snare
   - d. elapse

10. a terrible disaster
    - **a. calamity**
    - b. hygiene
    - c. swelter
    - d. aspiration

11. glowing or illuminated
    - a. gaunt
    - b. finite
    - **c. luminous**
    - d. irascible

12. to move at the same time or speed
    - **a. synchronize**
    - b. flinch
    - c. avenge
    - d. decompose

13. foolish or irrational
    - a. dilapidated
    - b. finicky
    - **c. absurd**
    - d. skeptical

14. to fill with fear
    - a. flinch
    - b. renounce
    - c. gorge
    - **d. dismay**

15. to refuse to give up
    - **a. persist**
    - b. exert
    - c. prohibit
    - d. elapse

16. getting results without wasting time or effort
    - a. unintelligible
    - b. luminous
    - c. sopping
    - **d. efficient**

17. to surrender something
a. renounce   b. synchronize   c. dishonor   d. nibble

18. a request for action
a. excursion   b. petition   c. calamity   d. catastrophe

19. the words of a song
a. niche   b. exhaust   c. lyrics   d. dialect

20. cannot be understood
a. intolerable   b. dilapidated   c. unintelligible   d. lithe

Sentence Completion
Choose the word from the box that best completes each of the following sentences. Write the word in the blank.

accessories	nibble	effect	quirks	upkeep
burnishes	hysteria	niche	upheavals	ruckus

1. The American Revolution is one of the most famous political ____upheavals____ in our history.

2. We calmed Mai's ____hysteria____ by assuring her that her leg was not broken.

3. The ____upkeep____ of the yard is my responsibility this summer.

4. Eating sugary foods can have a bad ____effect____ on your teeth.

5. Reflectors and a light are important ____accessories____ for any bike.

6. Lynn found her ____niche____ on the swimming team.

7. Once a year, Tom ____burnishes____ his first-place tennis trophy.

8. A ____ruckus____ erupted in the stands when our team won the championship.

9. "We all have our ____quirks____," Kirk said as he carefully folded and saved his gum wrapper.

10. I like to ____nibble____ on popcorn while I do my homework.

Fill in the Blanks

Fill in the bubble of the pair of words that best completes each sentence.

1. I was _____ about whether they could _____ such difficult moves in two short days.
   - (a.) skeptical, synchronize
   - (b.) finicky, avenge
   - (c.) persuasive, renounce
   - (d.) irascible, burnish

2. After the _____, the Earthquake Emergency Center was _____ by a flood of victims.
   - (a.) hysteria, dilapidated
   - (b.) catastrophe, inundated
   - (c.) diagnosis, prohibited
   - (d.) hypothesis, exhausted

3. The food was _____, even for a(n) _____ like me!
   - (a.) gaunt, ruckus
   - (b.) sopping, calamity
   - (c.) intolerable, glutton
   - (d.) absurd, excursion

4. _____ study habits will help you avoid a(n) _____ on next week's test.
   - (a.) Luminous, excursion
   - (b.) Unintelligible, upheaval
   - (c.) Efficient, calamity
   - (d.) Sopping, dialect

5. When Jamie is trying to _____ his influence, he can be very _____.
   - (a.) renounce, irascible
   - (b.) synchronize, unintelligible
   - (c.) exhaust, prevalent
   - (d.) exert, persuasive

6. The principal _____ activities that could cause _____ for our school.
   - (a.) decelerates, dismay
   - (b.) persists, retorts
   - (c.) prohibits, dishonor
   - (d.) avenges, curiosity

7. My younger sister raised a(n) _____ about buying the latest trendy _____.
   - (a.) ruckus, accessory
   - (b.) hysteria, upheaval
   - (c.) aspiration, dialect
   - (d.) petition, niche

8. The comedian's _____ was _____ to the audience.
   - (a.) hygiene, luminous
   - (b.) retort, unintelligible
   - (c.) dismay, skeptical
   - (d.) diagnosis, irascible

9. The toddler's _____ caused a(n) _____ in the theater.
   - (a.) nominee, quirk
   - (b.) curiosity, petition
   - (c.) hysteria, upheaval
   - (d.) accessory, retort

10. The _____ aftermath _____ the whole community.
    - (a.) glutton's, tainted
    - (b.) calamity's, astounded
    - (c.) niche's, snared
    - (d.) quirk's, dishonored

Classifying Words

Sort the words in the box by writing each word to complete a phrase in the correct category.

absurd	aspiration	catastrophe	curiosity	dilapidated
effect	elapse	excursions	finicky	glutton
hygiene	hypothesis	inundated	irascible	lyrics
nominee	persuasive	petition	skeptical	swelter

Words You Might Use to Talk About Habits and Quirks

1. has always been _____finicky_____ about eating vegetables
2. such lively _____curiosity_____ that she asks too many questions
3. joins in on the _____lyrics_____ of every song on the radio
4. practices good _____hygiene_____ so she always looks presentable
5. makes a(n) _____glutton_____ of himself when strawberries are in season

Words You Might Use to Talk About Vacations

6. visit the site of the historic _____catastrophe_____
7. take as many sight-seeing _____excursions_____ as we can
8. likes to sit on a hot beach and _____swelter_____
9. _____inundated_____ us with travel brochures
10. shops for antiques in old, _____dilapidated_____ barns

Words You Might Use to Talk About Solving Problems

11. says no idea should ever be called foolish or _____absurd_____
12. making a(n) _____hypothesis_____ about the cause of the problem
13. using words, not fists, to be _____persuasive_____
14. makes every attempt to avoid their _____irascible_____ classmate
15. letting some time _____elapse_____ before taking any action

Words You Might Use to Talk About a Political Campaign

16. votes for the best _____nominee_____ for the job
17. having the _____aspiration_____ of becoming president
18. feeling a little _____skeptical_____ about some of the candidates' promises
19. circulated a(n) _____petition_____ to put the issue on the ballot
20. thought about the _____effect_____ the candidate would have on our country

CHAPTER 4

WORD LIST

Read each word using the pronunciation key.

accuracy (ak´ yər ə sē)
bauble (bô´ bəl)
caustic (kô´ stik)
decry (di krī´)
dilemma (di lem´ ə)
disown (dis ōn´)
elimination (i lim ə nā´ shən)
external (ek stər´ nəl)
flippant (flip´ ənt)
grieve (grēv)
idolize (īd´ ə līz)
isolate (ī´ sə lāt)
maneuver (mə no͞o´ vər)
nonchalant (non shə länt´)
pillar (pil´ ər)
random (ran´ dəm)
rung (ruŋ)
speculate (spek´ yə lāt)
tangible (tan´ jə bəl)
upright (up´ rīt)

WORD STUDY

Prefixes

The prefix *trans-* means "across, over, through," or "beyond."

transatlantic (trans ət lan´ tik) *(adj.)* crossing or reaching across the Atlantic
transcend (tran send´) *(v.)* to rise above
transform (trans fôrm´) *(v.)* to change in form
translate (trans´ lāt) *(v.)* to change from one language into another
translucent (trans lo͞o´ sənt) *(adj.)* allowing light to pass through partially
transmit (trans mit´) *(v.)* to send, pass along, or communicate

Challenge Words

absolution (ab sə lo͞o´ shən)
erratic (i rat´ ik)
jocund (jok´ ənd)
magnanimous (mag nan´ ə məs)
tout (tout)

■ **TEACHER TIP:** See page ix for suggestions on how to use this page.

WORDS IN CONTEXT

Read each sentence below to figure out the meaning of the word in **bold**. Use reasoning skills and the remainder of the sentence to help you. Write the meaning of the word on the line.

1. Unable to resolve the **dilemma**, Matt and Ari turned to others for advice.

   a situation that requires a difficult choice

2. Liz hurt Ted's feelings with her **caustic** remark about his costume.

   harshly critical or sarcastic

3. As the milk streamed across the table, I ran to put the carton **upright**.

   in a standing, straight-up position

4. Ashley offered no **tangible** proof that Tony had cheated, so the principal had to believe that he had not.

   able to be seen or touched

5. The townspeople will surely **decry** any decision that might damage the forest.

   to criticize publicly

6. Ramón threw the darts with great **accuracy** and hit three bull's-eyes in a row.

   exactness

7. Kathy's father grounded her for two days for her **flippant** response to her uncle.

   lacking respect or seriousness

8. The baby likes to play with the **baubles** hanging around her mother's neck.

   small decorations or trinkets

9. Among the ruins of the ancient temple, only two stone **pillars** remain.

   a building column that supports something above, such as a roof

10. Brian will probably **grieve** the loss of his iguana for several weeks.

    to feel great sadness

WORD MEANINGS

Word Learning

Study the spelling, part(s) of speech, and meaning(s) of each word. Complete each sentence by writing the word on the line. Then read the sentence.

1. **accuracy** *(n.)* 1. the quality of being correct; 2. exactness

   I did not have much faith in the _____accuracy_____ of my guess.

2. **bauble** *(n.)* a small decoration or trinket

   My friend showed me the new _____bauble_____ on her wrist.

3. **caustic** *(adj.)* 1. capable of burning, dissolving, or causing other damage; 2. harshly critical or sarcastic

   Scientists often use _____caustic_____ chemicals in the lab.

4. **decry** *(v.)* 1. to criticize publicly; 2. to devalue

   We were surprised that they did not _____decry_____ the senator's plan.

5. **dilemma** *(n.)* a situation that requires a difficult choice

   Kristin faced the _____dilemma_____ of how she would do all that work in two weeks.

6. **disown** *(v.)* to refuse to accept as one's own

   Eddie might _____disown_____ the idea rather than take credit for it.

7. **elimination** *(n.)* removal

   They agreed upon the _____elimination_____ of three items from the menu.

8. **external** *(adj.)* on the outside or outer part

   The house is fine inside, but it has some _____external_____ flaws.

9. **flippant** *(adj.)* lacking respect or seriousness

   The others may not appreciate your _____flippant_____ attitude because they take the matter very seriously.

10. **grieve** *(v.)* 1. to feel great sadness; 2. to cause great sadness

    The hockey team began to _____grieve_____ when they learned the spring thaw had melted their hockey rink.

11. **idolize** *(v.)* 1. to view with admiration or devotion; 2. to worship

    I think she will always _____idolize_____ her mother.

12. **isolate** *(v.)* to separate from a group or whole

The zookeeper decided to _____**isolate**_____ the sick giraffe from the other animals.

13. **maneuver** *(n.)* a planned and skillful move; *(v.)* to make a skillful move

The skater made a graceful _____**maneuver**_____ on the ice.

I can't _____**maneuver**_____ the fishing pole very well while I'm sitting in the boat.

14. **nonchalant** *(adj.)* not concerned; indifferent

She appears _____**nonchalant**_____, but I know she is worried about the contest.

15. **pillar** *(n.)* 1. a building column that supports something above, such as a roof; 2. a person in an important position

A 20-foot _____**pillar**_____ stood at each corner of the pavilion.

16. **random** *(adj.)* 1. happening or done without a plan; 2. without order

Jackie lay the floor tiles in a _____**random**_____ fashion.

17. **rung** *(n.)* 1. a step of a ladder; 2. the piece of wood that spans two chair legs for support

Michael stood on the lowest _____**rung**_____ of the ladder.

18. **speculate** *(v.)* 1. to think carefully about or suppose; 2. to buy or sell something in hopes of making a profit

I _____**speculate**_____ that spring will come early this year.

19. **tangible** *(adj.)* able to be seen or touched

The decision had no _____**tangible**_____ effects.

20. **upright** *(adj.)* 1. in a standing, straight-up position; 2. morally good

She played the tunes on an old _____**upright**_____ piano.

Vocabulary in Action

You already know that a **dilemma** is a problem that offers at least two solutions, none of which are acceptable or ideal. A person who finds herself in a dilemma has been traditionally been described as being placed "on the horns of a dilemma;" that is, neither horn is very comfortable. There are many famous dilemmas. Here are a few you may want to learn more about: Cornelian dilemma, Euthyphro dilemma, Platonia dilemma, Hedgehog's dilemma, and Prisoner's dilemma.

Use Your Vocabulary

Choose the word from the Word List that best completes each sentence. Write the word on the line. You may use the plural form of nouns and the past tense of verbs if necessary.

An ordinary walk to a(n) __1__ creek ended up causing my friends and me to __2__. Instead of natural beauty, we found brown water and dead fish. At first, we sat down and __3__ the sad sight. Then we decided that __4__ of the problem was a better use of our time. We tossed out some __5__ ideas. We __6__ about what we should do. Then we traced our way back along the creek. Soon we came to a factory at the edge of the water. A(n) __7__ pipe ran down the building. It must have had a leak, because __8__ chemicals were pouring into the creek.

That's not the end of the story, though. Now I had a real __9__. The factory was the place where my father worked. Would Dad get in trouble? Would I? My friends and I tried to be __10__ as we asked for the boss, but inside we were shaking. We were afraid she would think we were just a bunch of __11__ troublemakers. She definitely did not! When she heard our story, she called for quick action. A man in protective clothing brought a ladder to the leaky pipe. He braced it between the creek bottom and a(n) __12__ __13__ on the side of the building. He stood on the ladder's bottom __14__ and went to work with skill and __15__. With a few quick __16__, he stopped the leak. My dad's boss breathed a sigh of relief and smiled at my friends and me. I wasn't afraid of her anymore. I __17__ her for her fast thinking.

But I was afraid Dad would __18__ me for all the trouble I'd caused. Instead, he greeted me that night with a big smile. He handed me a necklace with a tiny fish charm. I cherish that necklace. It is not just a(n) __19__. It is a(n) __20__ reminder of the day we saved the creek.

1. _____ isolated _____
2. _____ grieve _____
3. _____ decried _____
4. _____ elimination _____
5. _____ random _____
6. _____ speculated _____
7. _____ external _____
8. _____ caustic _____
9. _____ dilemma _____
10. _____ nonchalant _____
11. _____ flippant _____
12. _____ upright _____
13. _____ pillar _____
14. _____ rung _____
15. _____ accuracy _____
16. _____ maneuvers _____
17. _____ idolized _____
18. _____ disown _____
19. _____ bauble _____
20. _____ tangible _____

SYNONYMS

Synonyms are words that have the same or nearly the same meanings.

Part 1 Choose the word from the box that is the best synonym for each group of words. Write the word on the line.

caustic	grieve	decry	pillar
external	flippant	speculate	tangible

1. corroding, acidic, stinging, biting _____ caustic

2. mourn, sorrow, distress, pain _____ grieve

3. frivolous, offhand, light _____ flippant

4. consider, contemplate, to venture _____ speculate

5. post, pole, a leader _____ pillar

6. physical, real, concrete _____ tangible

7. denounce, condemn, to diminish _____ decry

8. outer, exterior _____ external

Part 2 Replace the underlined word with a word from the box that means the same or almost the same. Write your answer on the line.

upright	bauble	isolate	dilemma
random	disown	maneuver	

9. Matthew feared that his angry grandfather would <u>renounce</u> him.
   _____ disown

10. He has a very <u>honest</u> character. _____ upright

11. Every time Courtney tries to finish early, she runs into a <u>jam</u>.
    _____ dilemma

12. The veterinarian chose to <u>quarantine</u> all of the sick animals.
    _____ isolate

13. John hung a red <u>ornament</u> on the tree. _____ bauble

14. The swift military <u>operation</u> surprised the unsuspecting foes.

_____ maneuver

15. Always be on the lookout for a <u>chance</u> opportunity. _____ random

➡ ANTONYMS

Antonyms are words that have opposite or nearly opposite meanings.

Part 1 Choose the word from the box that is the best antonym for each group of words. Write the word on the line.

decry	disown	external
idolize	isolate	random

1. claim, accept as one's own _____ disown

2. compliment, admire, value _____ decry

3. join, unite, combine _____ isolate

4. deliberate, planned, intentional _____ random

5. despise, scorn, disdain _____ idolize

6. inner, internal _____ external

Part 2 Replace the underlined word with a word from the box that means the opposite or almost the opposite. Write your answer on the line.

accuracy	flippant	grieve	nonchalant	caustic

7. Jimmy's departure caused everyone to <u>celebrate</u>. _____ grieve

8. We were all surprised by Andy's <u>solemn</u> response to the tragedy.

_____ flippant

9. Susanna appeared quite <u>emotional</u> when her sister walked into the room.

_____ nonchalant

10. Jody's <u>soothing</u> words did not make me feel much better. _____ caustic

11. I completed the test with a high level of <u>error</u>. _____ accuracy

WORD STUDY

Prefixes Choose a word from the box that belongs with each group of words. Write the word on the line.

transatlantic	transcend	transform
translate	translucent	transmit

1. lampshade, screen   translucent

2. difficulties, cultural boundaries   transcend

3. memo, message   transmit

4. flight, relationship, business   transatlantic

5. language, computer program   translate

6. object, personality, attitude   transform

Vocabulary in Action

See if you can spot the Challenge Word in this poem by William Wordsworth. To what does the word refer in this poem?

The Daffodils
by William Wordsworth

I wandered lonely as a cloud
   That floats on high o'er vales and hills,
When all at once I saw a crowd,
   A host, of golden daffodils;
Beside the lake, beneath the trees,
fluttering and dancing in the breeze.

Continuous as the stars that shine
   And twinkle on the Milky Way,
They stretched in never-ending line
   Along the margin of a bay:
Ten thousand saw I at a glance,
Tossing their heads in sprightly dance.

The waves beside them danced, but they
   Out-did the sparkling waves in glee:
A Poet could not but be gay,
   In such a jocund company:
I gazed—and gazed—but little thought
What wealth the show to me had brought:

For oft, when on my couch I lie
   In vacant or in pensive mood,
They flash upon that inward eye
   Which is the bliss of solitude;
And then my heart with pleasure fills,
And dances with the daffodils.

CHALLENGE WORDS

Word Learning—Challenge!

Study the spelling, part of speech, and meaning(s) of each word. Complete each sentence by writing the word on the line. Then read the sentence.

1. **absolution** *(n.)* 1. forgiveness; 2. freeing from punishment

   She asked the judge for the _____absolution_____ of her jail sentence.

2. **erratic** *(adj.)* 1. irregular in action; 2. odd

   We have heard only _____erratic_____ reports of the situation.

3. **jocund** *(adj.)* merry, cheerful, or jolly

   We all like Aunt Lilly's _____jocund_____ good humor.

4. **magnanimous** *(adj.)* showing a generous or noble spirit

   His _____magnanimous_____ offer to give up the house touched us all.

5. **tout** *(v.)* to recommend or praise something highly

   If you ask Terry which computer to buy, she will always _____tout_____ her most expensive product.

Use Your Vocabulary—Challenge!

Oil Spill There has been an oil spill off the coast of Alaska. You and your friends join the rescue efforts to save the wildlife. Write a story about your rescue operation. Use the Challenge Words above.

Vocabulary in Action

Prefixes and suffixes change the meaning of words and how they function in sentences. Studying words and adding prefixes and suffixes will boost your vocabulary. Look at the vocabulary word *transcend* from this chapter. *Transcend* is a transitive verb that means "to rise above or go beyond the limits of." If you add the suffix *-ent*, you create the word *transcendent*. This adjective describes a person or thing that exceeds usual limits. If you add the suffix *-ence*, you get *transcendence*, a noun that names the quality or state of being transcendent. Other variations on the verb *transcend* include *transcendently* and *transcendental*. Study the other words from this chapter and see how many words you can make from them.

FUN WITH WORDS

In chemistry, letters are used to represent different chemicals and elements. Equations such as the one below show how elements combine to form compounds:

$$2H_2 + O_2 = 2H_2O$$

This shows how hydrogen (H) and oxygen (O) can be combined to make water.

In word chemistry, you'll see an equation like the one above. The letters in each equation combine to make a vocabulary word. A small number to the right of a letter tells you how many times that letter appears in the word. The clue next to the equation gives you a hint. For example:

$ELA + B_2U$ = a bright, shiny thing _____ bauble _____

The small 2 tells you there are two b's in this vocabulary word. Determine how many letters are actually in the word. Then rearrange them and write the answer on the line. The answer to the example is **bauble**.

1. $E_2R + IVG$ = to feel sad   _____ grieve _____

2. $RL_2I + AP$ = a support   _____ pillar _____

3. $C_2TS + UAI$ = able to cause damage   _____ caustic _____

4. $UC_3A_2 + YR$ = exactness   _____ accuracy _____

5. $N_3LA_2 + TCOH$ = indifferent   _____ nonchalant _____

6. $I_3N_2AE + ML + OT$ = removal   _____ elimination _____

7. $ZI_2D + O_4LE - O_3$ = to worship   _____ idolize _____

8. $N_3UG_4R_4 - N_2R_3G_3$ = a step of a ladder   _____ rung _____

CHAPTER 5

WORD LIST

WORD STUDY

Read each word using the pronunciation key.

acquit (ə kwit´)
belligerent (bə lij´ ər ənt)
censor (sen´ sər)
defiance (di fī´ əns)
diligence (dil´ i jəns)
dispatch (dis pach´)
embankment (em baŋk´ mənt)
facet (fas´ it)
flourish (flər´ ish)
grudge (gruj)
ilk (ilk)
itemize (ī´ tə mīz)
mediocre (mē dē ō´ kər)
notable (nō´ tə bəl)
pivot (piv´ ət)
rascal (ras´ kəl)
sage (sāj)
sprightly (sprīt´ lē)
taut (tôt)
vacuum (vak´ yo͞om)

Suffixes

The suffixes -*ous* and -*ious* mean "characterized by."

ambitious (am bi´ shəs) *(adj.)* characterized by ambition; eager to succeed
glorious (glôr´ ē əs) *(adj.)* characterized by glory or splendor
malicious (mə li´ shəs) *(adj.)* characterized by malice, or ill will
nauseous (nô´ shəs) *(adj.)* characterized by nausea, or sickness
nervous (nər´ vəs) *(adj.)* characterized by nerves or anxiety
voracious (vô rā´ shəs) *(adj.)* characterized by a great appetite

Challenge Words

chide (chīd)
contentious (kən ten´ chəs)
filibuster (fil´ ə bus tər)
hypothetical (hī pə thet´ i kəl)
invincible (in vin´ sə bəl)

■ **TEACHER TIP:** See page ix for suggestions on how to use this page.

Read each sentence below to figure out the meaning of the word in **bold**. Use reasoning skills and the remainder of the sentence to help you. Write the meaning of the word on the line.

1. Matt held the tent ropes **taut** so Deanna could hammer the stakes into the ground.

   pulled or drawn tight

2. Keith and his studious friends are all of the same **ilk**.

   type or kind

3. A lot of people like that new restaurant, but I found the food **mediocre** at best.

   not good or bad; commonplace

4. Famous actors, **notable** journalists, and politicians filled the audience.

   prominent

5. Confucius was a **sage** of ancient China whose sayings are still repeated today.

   a wise person

6. Michael's departure created a **vacuum** that was not easy to fill.

   an absence or emptiness

7. Notice how the **facets** of the gem reflect the sunlight.

   small, flat surfaces on a tooth, stone, or gem

8. Don't hold a **grudge** against me just because I told your secret.

   a strong feeling of ill will or resentment

9. A lot of inspiration and much **diligence** helped Thomas Edison achieve his status as a great inventor.

   persistence

10. Armadillos are everywhere; they **flourish** in warm, dry parts of the country.

    to grow well or thrive

WORD MEANINGS

Word Learning

Study the spelling, part(s) of speech, and meaning(s) of each word. Complete each sentence by writing the word on the line. Then read the sentence.

1. **acquit** *(v.)* to find not guilty or free from a charge

   Lack of evidence led the jury to _____acquit_____ him of the crime.

2. **belligerent** *(adj.)* 1. ready to fight; angry; 2. at war

   She received a _____belligerent_____ letter from her neighbors, demanding that she mow her lawn.

3. **censor** *(n.)* a person who examines materials to remove parts that do not meet a set of standards; *(v.)* to examine for the purpose of removing material that does not meet a set of standards

   The _____censor_____ removed everything having to do with crime.

   According to the First Amendment, the government may not _____censor_____ the press.

4. **defiance** *(n.)* a resistance to authority or an opposing force

   Yolanda stood up in _____defiance_____ of the bully to defend her sister.

5. **diligence** *(n.)* 1. careful attention to one's job; 2. persistence

   When Josh saw the A on his test, he knew that his _____diligence_____ had paid off.

6. **dispatch** *(v.)* to send off; *(n.)* 1. act of sending off; 2. speed; 3. a quickly sent written message

   The general will _____dispatch_____ an order to cease firing.

   We received the general's _____dispatch_____ this morning.

7. **embankment** *(n.)* a mound of earth used to prevent flooding or to support a roadway

   When the car hit the icy patch, it swerved up on the _____embankment_____.

8. **facet** *(n.)* 1. the small, flat surface on a tooth, stone, or gem; 2. a part or phase

   That is a _____facet_____ of her personality I have never seen.

9. **flourish** *(v.)* to grow well or thrive

   Despite the lack of nuts and seeds, the squirrels continue to _____flourish_____.

10. **grudge** *(v.)* to hesitate to give or admit something; *(n.)* a strong feeling of ill will or resentment

They did not _____grudge_____ me the prize I deserved.

She has always held a _____grudge_____ against me.

11. **ilk** *(n.)* type or kind

Because she lies, I don't want her _____ilk_____ hanging around here.

12. **itemize** *(v.)* to list one by one

Please _____itemize_____ the supplies in the art room.

13. **mediocre** *(adj.)* 1. not good or bad; 2. commonplace

That theater group only produces _____mediocre_____ plays.

14. **notable** *(adj.)* 1. worthy of notice or remarkable; 2. prominent; *(n.)* a person who is worthy of notice

Aside from a broken window, the fire caused no _____notable_____ damage.

At the meeting, we saw Ms. Broucek, a _____notable_____ in city politics.

15. **pivot** *(n.)* a rod or shaft around which some other part rotates or swings; *(v.)* to rotate or swing

Do you want me to fix the broken _____pivot_____ on this swing set?

The gymnast will _____pivot_____ before she reaches the end of the mat.

16. **rascal** *(n.)* a mischievous person or animal

It looks like some furry _____rascal_____ has gotten into the trash.

17. **sage** *(adj.)* wise or showing keen judgment; *(n.)* 1. a wise person; 2. an herb used for cooking

I appreciate your _____sage_____ advice.

Mom brought some fresh _____sage_____ home from Billy's garden.

18. **sprightly** *(adj.)* lively, active, or animated

His _____sprightly_____ step showed me that his mood had improved.

19. **taut** *(adj.)* 1. pulled or drawn tight; 2. emotionally or mentally strained or tense

You have to pull the canvas _____taut_____ over the frame.

20. **vacuum** *(n.)* 1. a completely empty space; 2. an absence or emptiness; 3. a machine for cleaning by use of suction; *(adj.)* containing air or other gas at reduced pressure

The president's resignation has created a leadership _____vacuum_____.

The company sells _____vacuum_____-packed coffee.

Use Your Vocabulary

Choose the word from the Word List that best completes each sentence. Write the word on the line. You may use the plural form of nouns and the past tense of verbs if necessary.

I am known in my neighborhood as the __1__ of Bassett Lane. I earned that title by solving mysteries. One day my friend Brady __2__ an urgent message. His new sweater was missing, and he needed to find it.

"That sweater was a gift from Grandma," he said in a(n) __3__ voice. "If I don't wear it, her feelings will be hurt."

"That sweater did not just disappear into a(n) __4__," I said. "When did you last have it?"

Brady couldn't remember, so I asked him to __5__ the places he had been. Finally, he recalled leaving it on a chair in his room. I searched the room with __6__. It was very clean, but I did manage to find a few long golden hairs and some tiny pieces of dried mud near the chair. Brady's room, I thought, looked __7__. It was not filled with interesting things like mine. But he did have one __8__ decoration. It was a large framed photo of a beautiful dog. "Is that your dog?" I asked.

"Yes," he said proudly. "That's my golden retriever, Toby."

I did not __9__ my words. "Toby is the criminal," I declared.

"No way!" Brady answered in a(n) __10__ voice, but he followed when I __11__ and headed out the door. Outside, I saw muddy paw prints. We followed them down the __12__ in the backyard, moving at a(n) __13__ pace. Soon we saw Toby lying in front of a small hollow in the bank. Toby stood up with an air of __14__, but when he moved aside, we could see a ball, an old shoe, and other things of that __15__. "Toby's life of crime has __16__," I laughed. "If you look in there, you will find your sweater." And of course, Brady did.

Toby has not been __17__, but luckily Brady doesn't hold a(n) __18__. He knows playfulness is a(n) __19__ of Toby's personality. "You __20__," he said, petting Toby's head. "From now on, I'll remember to put my things away."

1. _____ sage
2. _____ dispatched
3. _____ taut
4. _____ vacuum
5. _____ itemize
6. _____ diligence
7. _____ mediocre
8. _____ notable
9. _____ censor
10. _____ belligerent
11. _____ pivoted
12. _____ embankment
13. _____ sprightly
14. _____ defiance
15. _____ ilk
16. _____ flourished
17. _____ acquitted
18. _____ grudge
19. _____ facet
20. _____ rascal

SYNONYMS

Synonyms are words that have the same or nearly the same meanings.

Part 1 Choose the word from the box that is the best synonym for each group of words. Write the word on the line.

defiance	diligence	dispatch	flourish
itemize	mediocre	rascal	taut

1. transmit, bulletin, quickness _____dispatch_____

2. list, detail, catalog _____itemize_____

3. rigid, strained, stretched _____taut_____

4. prankster, scoundrel, scamp _____rascal_____

5. ordinary, normal, average _____mediocre_____

6. prosper, succeed _____flourish_____

7. opposition, disobedience, contempt _____defiance_____

8. persistence, industriousness, effort _____diligence_____

Part 2 Replace the underlined word with a word from the box that means the same or almost the same. Write your answer on the line.

belligerent	acquit	censor	sprightly
sage	notable	grudge	

9. The basketball coach chose Melissa for her <u>extraordinary</u> strength.
_____notable_____

10. He blamed the problem on his <u>aggressive</u> neighbors. _____belligerent_____

11. Zeke always consulted the old <u>philosopher</u> for advice. _____sage_____

12. The two families don't speak to each other because of a long-standing <u>argument</u>.
_____grudge_____

13. Do you think the judiciary council will <u>pardon</u> her? _____acquit_____

14. My grandfather is a <u>spry</u> old man. _____sprightly_____

15. The film's obscene language did not get past the <u>inspector</u>. _____censor_____

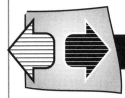 **ANTONYMS**

Antonyms are words that have opposite or nearly opposite meanings.

Part 1 Choose the word from the box that is the best antonym for each group of words. Write the word on the line.

acquit	flourish	sage	taut	sprightly

1. dull, lethargic, lifeless _____sprightly_____

2. slack, flexible, loose _____taut_____

3. fade, decline, fail _____flourish_____

4. fool, idiot; stupid, senseless _____sage_____

5. charge, blame, indict _____acquit_____

Part 2 Replace the underlined word with a word from the box that means the opposite or almost the opposite. Write your answer on the line.

belligerent	diligence	mediocre	notable

6. Yesterday we saw the <u>outstanding</u> doll exhibit at the museum.
_____mediocre_____

7. She always comes to meetings with a <u>friendly</u> attitude. _____belligerent_____

8. Marco displayed great <u>carelessness</u> in all of his work. _____diligence_____

9. Medgar Evers was a <u>regular</u> figure in the civil rights movement.
_____notable_____

WORD STUDY

Suffixes Choose the word from the box that might be used to describe each person or event. Write the word on the line.

ambitious	glorious	malicious
nauseous	nervous	voracious

1. someone auditioning for a school play   nervous

2. a passenger on a bumpy boat ride   nauseous

3. someone sitting down to Thanksgiving dinner   voracious

4. the birth of a child   glorious

5. a villain   malicious

6. a political campaign   ambitious

Vocabulary in Action

Look at each word on the Word Study list and try to figure out its noun form. For example, *ambition* is the nominative form of the word ***ambitious.*** Pay attention to how spelling is affected when you change the way a word functions in a sentence.

CHALLENGE WORDS

Word Learning—Challenge!

Study the spelling, part of speech, and meaning of each word. Complete each sentence by writing the word on the line. Then read the sentence.

1. **chide** *(v.)* to voice disapproval in a mild way

   My father always used to _____ chide _____ me for my impatience.

2. **contentious** *(adj.)* quick to argue or quarrel

   Those kids are a _____ contentious _____ bunch.

3. **filibuster** *(v.)* to attempt to keep a bill from passing in a legislature by the use of excessive speeches

   If it looks like the bill is going to pass, the senator will _____ filibuster _____.

4. **hypothetical** *(adj.)* based on an unproved idea

   Tell me about this _____ hypothetical _____ life on Mars.

5. **invincible** *(adj.)* incapable of being overcome or beaten

   The girls on the soccer team consider themselves _____ invincible _____.

Use Your Vocabulary—Challenge!

Mock Trial Your best friend has been accused of a crime he or she did not commit. You and your classmates hold a mock trial to see if your friend is guilty. On a separate sheet of paper, write about the events that happen. Include the five Challenge Words above. Use your imagination!

> ### Vocabulary in Action
>
> A **filibuster**, or "talking out a bill," is a form of obstruction in a legislature or other decision-making body. The term first came into use in the United States Senate. Senate rules permit a senator to speak for as long as he or she wishes on any topic. A supermajority of three-fifths of the Senate is required to stop a filibuster.
>
> Perhaps the most famous example of a filibuster in American cinema comes from the 1939 film *Mr. Smith Goes to Washington*. At the movie's climax, a young senator—Jefferson Smith, played by Jimmy Stewart—stages a filibuster after he discovers that his mentor is corrupt.

FUN WITH WORDS

Each sentence contains a word from the Word list. As you read each question, think about what you can do to make the world a better place. Write your answers on the lines.

1. What do you think is the most *notable* part of our planet?

_____

_____

_____

2. What can you do to help our planet *flourish*?

_____

_____

_____

3. What *facets* of our world would you change? Why?

_____

_____

_____

4. *Itemize* at least five things that you enjoy about the world we live in.

_____

_____

_____

5. If you could *dispatch* a message to people in the past, what would you ask them to do to protect the world we live in today?

_____

_____

_____

_____

CHAPTER 6

WORD LIST

Read each word using the pronunciation key.

admissible (ad mis´ ə bəl)
beneficial (ben ə fish´ əl)
colleague (kol´ ēg)
deflate (di flāt´)
dilute (dī lōot´)
dispense (di spens´)
emotional (i mō´ shə nəl)
fallow (fal´ ō)
fluted (flōo´ tid)
haphazard (hap haz´ ərd)
illustrious (i lus´ trē əs)
jaunt (jônt)
merit (mâr´ it)
notorious (nō tôr´ ē əs)
platform (plat´ fôrm)
ratify (rat´ ə fī)
saline (sā´ lēn)
squander (skwon´ dər)
tenacity (tə nas´ ə tē)
venture (ven´ chər)

WORD STUDY

Homophones

Homophones are words that sound alike but have different spellings and meanings. Study the pairs of homophones below.

altar (ôl´ tər) *(n.)* a platform or raised area, as in a church
alter (ôl´ tər) *(v.)* to change

raise (rāz´) *(v.)* 1. to lift something; 2. to grow or breed something
raze (rāz´) *(v.)* to demolish

reek (rēk´) *(n.)* a terrible smell; *(v.)* to smell terrible
wreak (rēk´) *(v.)* to cause

Challenge Words

angst (äŋkst)
egocentric (ē gō sen´ trik)
fluctuate (fluk´ chōo āt)
obtrusive (əb trōo´ siv)
vindicate (vin´ di kāt)

■ **TEACHER TIP:** See page ix for suggestions on how to use this page.

WORDS IN CONTEXT

Read each sentence below to figure out the meaning of the word in **bold**. Use reasoning skills and the remainder of the sentence to help you. Write the meaning of the word on the line.

1. Your aunt is a senator? I never knew you had such **illustrious** relatives.

   well-known, famous

2. Representatives from both countries met today to **ratify** the new trade agreement.

   to approve for use or action

3. As I watched the pilot **deflate** the hot-air balloon, I thought about how much fun I'd had up in the air.

   to release air or gas from

4. I'm sure you've heard of Mr. Lane, the man who is **notorious** for his bad jokes.

   well-known, usually for unfavorable reasons

5. Use water to **dilute** the concentrated juice.

   to thin or weaken by adding liquid

6. He warned his sister not to **squander** her summer earnings on ice cream and movies.

   to spend wastefully

7. Janice waited impatiently on the **platform** for her brother's train.

   the deck of a train station

8. The fisherman's **tenacity** finally paid off when he caught the big fish after standing knee-deep in water all day.

   firmness, persistence, or determination

9. The **saline** solution in the beaker is for the next experiment.

   of, relating to, or containing salt

10. With Halloween pranksters everywhere, Kyle knew better than to **venture** outside the house.

    to undertake a risk

WORD MEANINGS

Word Learning

Study the spelling, part(s) of speech, and meaning(s) of each word. Complete each sentence by writing the word on the line. Then read the sentence.

1. **admissible** *(adj.)* 1. acceptable; 2. worthy of being permitted

   A hunch is not considered _____admissible_____ evidence.

2. **beneficial** *(adj.)* 1. making better or having benefit; 2. helpful

   Would it be _____beneficial_____ to talk to other people who know about this?

3. **colleague** *(n.)* a fellow worker

   Harold was my _____colleague_____ when I worked for the law firm.

4. **deflate** *(v.)* 1. to release air or gas from; 2. to reduce confidence or value

   If you tell her the bad news, you will _____deflate_____ her hopes completely.

5. **dilute** *(v.)* to thin or weaken by adding liquid; *(adj.)* weakened

   What should I use to _____dilute_____ this paint?

   We used a very _____dilute_____ solution for the experiment.

6. **dispense** *(v.)* 1. to give out or distribute; 2. to release from a duty

   I can't get the machine to _____dispense_____ the candy properly.

7. **emotional** *(adj.)* with strong feeling

   Our principal delivered a very _____emotional_____ graduation speech.

8. **fallow** *(adj.)* 1. plowed or tilled but not seeded for one growing season;
   2. uncultivated; *(n.)* earth that is plowed but not seeded

   We won't plant our _____fallow_____ land until next year.

   Sara and Mark are out plowing the _____fallow_____ today.

9. **fluted** *(adj.)* decorated with grooves

   For my birthday, I received a lovely pair of _____fluted_____ water glasses.

10. **haphazard** *(adj.)* by chance or without planning

    Her _____haphazard_____ attempts to organize the room were unsuccessful.

11. **illustrious** *(adj.)* well-known, famous

    The princess and her _____illustrious_____ guests danced all night long.

12. **jaunt** *(n.)* a short trip

    I'll just take a _____jaunt_____ down to the beach.

13. **merit** *(n.)* a valuable quality or trait; *(v.)* to earn or deserve

    These scholarships are based on _____merit_____.

    I thought he did not _____merit_____ such fine praise.

14. **notorious** *(adj.)* well-known, usually for unfavorable reasons

    Have you seen the _____notorious_____ robber?

15. **platform** *(n.)* 1. a raised surface; 2. the deck of a train station; 3. the ideas of a political candidate or party

    City parking reform is an important part of the candidate's _____platform_____.

16. **ratify** *(v.)* to approve for use or action

    Congress did not _____ratify_____ the new amendment to the Constitution.

17. **saline** *(adj.)* of, relating to, or containing salt

    We cannot drink the ocean's _____saline_____ waters.

18. **squander** *(v.)* to spend wastefully

    She feared that her son would _____squander_____ all of his hard-earned money.

19. **tenacity** *(n.)* firmness, persistence, or determination

    Eleanor showed _____tenacity_____ and grit when she chose to stay on the farm alone through the entire winter.

20. **venture** *(n.)* 1. a task that is risky or dangerous; 2. an undertaking involving chance; *(v.)* 1. to expose to danger; 2. to risk or to brave; 3. to offer at risk of rejection

    Marty lost some money in that business _____venture_____.

    I don't even want to _____venture_____ a guess about what happened.

Use Your Vocabulary

Choose the word from the Word List that best completes each sentence. Write the word on the line. You may use the plural form of nouns and the past tense of verbs if necessary.

When it came time to organize the spring dance, few students __1__ to get involved. We were all glad when Kendra decided to take charge. She had the __2__ to whip the student council into shape. The council was __3__ for sitting like a(n) __4__ field and producing very little. We had pulled off the last dance in a very __5__ fashion, and no one had much fun. Kendra leaped into her role as the boss and set up an operating budget for the dance.

"We can't __6__ our limited funds," she said. "We don't need a machine to __7__ the drinks. We'll just make lemonade in pitchers." She thought it __8__ to organize very carefully. We found her plan __9__ and __10__ all of her proposals.

Jake, one of our __11__ on Student Council, suggested the theme of ancient Greece. We borrowed some __12__ plastic columns from the drama club and transformed the gym into an ancient Greek temple. We built a(n) __13__ at one end of the gym, where two students would be crowned as Apollo and Athena.

We all came to school early on the big day to start blowing up balloons. I was a little concerned that they might __14__ over the course of the day, but they didn't. Late in the day, Kendra sent Mandy on a(n) __15__ to the store to pick up the lemonade. When Mandy returned, she __16__ the concentrate with water and took a sip. She made a horrible face. "Oh no! This is too sour!" she cried out. Mandy tended to get fairly __17__ about things.

"Don't worry," said Kendra. "I saw a bowl of sugar in the cafeteria." She brought back a bowl of white crystallized powder and dumped it into the punch bowl. Mandy had another sip, and made an even more horrible face. I tried it myself, and it had a distinctly __18__ taste.

"Kendra," I said. "That bowl was full of salt!"

Salty lemonade aside, the dance was a success. All agreed that Kendra __19__ great praise for putting together the most __20__ event of the school year.

1. _____ ventured
2. _____ tenacity
3. _____ notorious
4. _____ fallow
5. _____ haphazard
6. _____ squander
7. _____ dispense
8. _____ beneficial
9. _____ admissible
10. _____ ratified
11. _____ colleagues
12. _____ fluted
13. _____ platform
14. _____ deflate
15. _____ jaunt
16. _____ diluted
17. _____ emotional
18. _____ saline
19. _____ merited
20. _____ illustrious

SYNONYMS

Synonyms are words that have the same or nearly the same meanings.

Part 1 Choose the word from the box that is the best synonym for each group of words. Write the word on the line.

admissible	colleague	dilute	haphazard
jaunt	merit	ratify	venture

1. random, unplanned, not systematic   _haphazard_

2. worth, quality; be entitled to   _merit_

3. allowable, legitimate   _admissible_

4. endorse, support, agree to   _ratify_

5. excursion, trip   _jaunt_

6. watered down; make less thick   _dilute_

7. associate, teammate, partner   _colleague_

8. hazard; imperil, endanger   _venture_

Part 2 Replace the underlined word(s) with a word from the box that means the same or almost the same. Write your answer on the line.

fallow	notorious	emotional	platform
illustrious	beneficial	squander	

9. We held our rally on a huge wooden <u>stage</u>. _platform_

10. I am honored to have such a(n) <u>celebrated</u> author in our midst.
    illustrious

11. He proceeded to <u>throw away</u> his money on expensive cars and extravagant vacations.
    squander

12. It would be <u>advantageous</u> to research your options before making a purchase.
    beneficial

13. I found myself in the midst of a(n) <u>passionate</u> debate. _emotional_

14. Her mind lay <u>inactive</u> for many years. _____ fallow _____

15. I dreaded the <u>infamous</u> Midwestern winter. _____ notorious _____

ANTONYMS

Antonyms are words that have opposite or nearly opposite meanings.

Part 1 Choose the word from the box that is the best antonym for each group of words. Write the word on the line.

| merit | venture | squander | haphazard | beneficial |

1. safety, security; protect _____ venture _____

2. organized, methodical, designed _____ haphazard _____

3. useless, harmful, detrimental _____ beneficial _____

4. fault, defect; not to be worthy of _____ merit _____

5. save, use wisely _____ squander _____

Part 2 Replace the underlined word with a word from the box that means the opposite or almost the opposite. Write your answer on the line.

| tenacity | emotional | ratify | admissible | dilute |

6. The committee would not <u>veto</u> the proposal. _____ ratify _____

7. The illness really did <u>intensify</u> her strength. _____ dilute _____

8. I have never heard such an <u>unfeeling</u> argument for kindness to animals.
_____ emotional _____

9. As our leader, he showed more <u>indecision</u> than usual. _____ tenacity _____

10. The university judged the research findings <u>unacceptable</u>. _____ admissible _____

WORD STUDY

Homophones Choose the word from the box that best completes each of the following sentences.

raise	alter	wreak
raze	altar	reek

1. She refuses to _____ alter _____ the way she does things.

2. Tom's locker began to _____ reek _____ on Monday because he left his gym shoes in it over the weekend.

3. The workers will _____ raze _____ the barn that was destroyed by the fire.

4. Spilled liquids will _____ wreak _____ havoc with the computer keyboard.

5. The newly married couple walked all the way around the _____ altar _____.

6. If you call her name, she will _____ raise _____ her head.

Vocabulary in Action

The word **angst**, a Germanic word meaning "fear" or "anxiety," is a fairly new addition to the English language. British writer George Eliot used the word as early as 1849, and it was popularized in English by translations of Sigmund Freud's work. But *angst* was not considered an English word until the 1940s. It is used in English to describe "an intense feeling of emotional strife." The German definition of *angst* is "the fear of possible suffering and a behavior resulting from uncertainty and strain which is caused by pain, loss, or death." In German, angst is different from fear in that fear usually refers to a material threat while angst is a nondirectional emotion.

CHALLENGE WORDS

Word Learning—Challenge!

Study the spelling, part of speech, and meaning(s) of each word. Complete each sentence by writing the word on the line. Then read the sentence.

1. **angst** *(n.)* anxiety or apprehension

   Travis thought about the upcoming events with great _____angst_____.

2. **egocentric** *(n.)* 1. being concerned with the individual rather than society; 2. self-centered; selfish

   I find her _____egocentric_____ and difficult to work with.

3. **fluctuate** *(v.)* 1. to continually change between two choices; 2. to vary

   Gasoline prices will probably continue to _____fluctuate_____.

4. **obtrusive** *(adj.)* calling attention to manner or conduct in an undesirable way

   Your _____obtrusive_____ remarks are making it hard for us to discuss this rationally.

5. **vindicate** *(v.)* 1. to free from blame; 2. to justify; 3. to uphold

   If I can prove I was right, I am hoping to _____vindicate_____ myself.

Use Your Vocabulary—Challenge!

Committee Plans Now it's time for your school to plan a week-long festival of sports and cultural events. But the members of the student planning committee cannot decide how to run things. Use the five Challenge Words above to write a story describing the events leading up to the festival.

> ## Vocabulary in Action
>
> Did you know that the word *homonym* comes from the conjunction of the Greek prefix *homo-*, meaning "same," and the suffix *-onym*, meaning "name"? Thus, it refers to two or more distinct words sharing the "same name."

FUN WITH WORDS

Complete the crossword puzzle using words from the Word List.

Across

3. showing feelings
6. acceptable
7. tilled but not seeded
8. famous
10. determination
11. to reduce confidence
12. to weaken
13. a quick trip

Down

1. to deserve
2. infamous
4. an associate
5. to approve
7. with grooves
9. salty

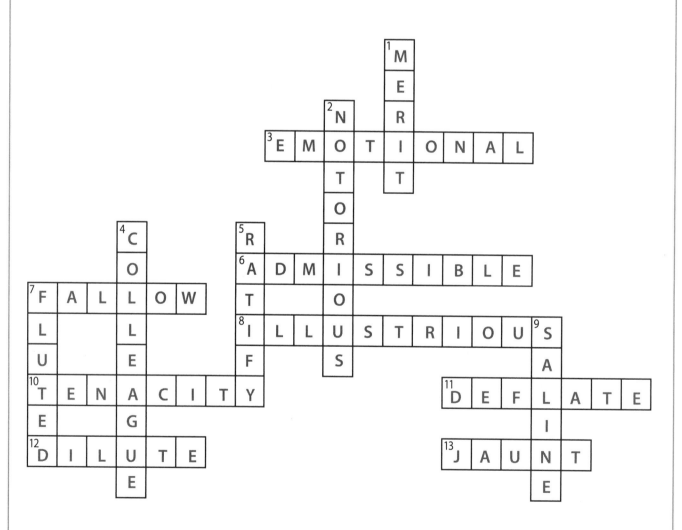

Review 4–6

Word Meanings
Fill in the bubble of the word that is best defined by each phrase.

1. not planned
   - (a.) haphazard
   - (b.) notorious
   - (c.) mediocre
   - (d.) flippant

2. to use wastefully
   - (a.) deflate
   - (b.) squander
   - (c.) decry
   - (d.) grieve

3. a learned person
   - (a.) embankment
   - (b.) sage
   - (c.) colleague
   - (d.) rascal

4. to clear from an accusation
   - (a.) itemize
   - (b.) disown
   - (c.) dispatch
   - (d.) acquit

5. celebrated and noted
   - (a.) caustic
   - (b.) emotional
   - (c.) illustrious
   - (d.) sprightly

6. to officially approve and confirm
   - (a.) speculate
   - (b.) ratify
   - (c.) dispense
   - (d.) deflate

7. to prosper
   - (a.) flourish
   - (b.) grieve
   - (c.) isolate
   - (d.) itemize

8. to direct or enact skillfully
   - (a.) idolize
   - (b.) maneuver
   - (c.) pivot
   - (d.) squander

9. not outstanding
   - (a.) external
   - (b.) fallow
   - (c.) dilute
   - (d.) mediocre

10. carefree and unconcerned
    - (a.) upright
    - (b.) taut
    - (c.) nonchalant
    - (d.) haphazard

11. elevated flooring
    - (a.) pillar
    - (b.) embankment
    - (c.) platform
    - (d.) dilemma

12. a showy ornament of little value
    - (a.) bauble
    - (b.) sage
    - (c.) vacuum
    - (d.) elimination

13. to be reluctant to give
    - (a.) censor
    - (b.) merit
    - (c.) grudge
    - (d.) disown

14. can be allowed
    - (a.) flippant
    - (b.) beneficial
    - (c.) admissible
    - (d.) emotional

15. a class or sort of something
    - (a.) facet
    - (b.) ilk
    - (c.) colleague
    - (d.) tenacity

16. hostile and inclined to fight
    - (a.) saline
    - (b.) emotional
    - (c.) external
    - (d.) belligerent

17. to disapprove strongly

    (a.) ratify   (b.) isolate   **(c.) decry**   (d.) venture

18. a brief outing

    (a.) jaunt   (b.) grudge   (c.) dispatch   (d.) diligence

19. that which can be touched

    (a.) illustrious   (b.) fluted   (c.) random   **(d.) tangible**

20. a vertical support structure

    (a.) pillar   (b.) bauble   (c.) accuracy   (d.) rung

Sentence Completion Choose the word from the box that best completes each of the following sentences. Write the word in the blank.

dilute	dilemma	dispensed	upright	censored
facets	defiance	random	notable	merits

1. Leticia faced a(n) _____dilemma_____ when two people asked her to the dance.

2. Our local museum contains many _____notable_____ sculptures.

3. Scientists could find no pattern to the animals' behavior, so they concluded the bears' actions must be _____random_____.

4. During World War II, all mail to and from soldiers was _____censored_____ to make sure no national secrets were being revealed.

5. Jack _____dispensed_____ the supplies and showed us how to pack them.

6. The many _____facets_____ of the stone reflected the light.

7. Tom's hard work on the play's stage _____merits_____ recognition.

8. Because the tent was small, Jan found it impossible to stand _____upright_____.

9. _____Defiance_____ of the rules will get you in trouble.

10. A(n) _____dilute_____ solution of vinegar and water makes a good cleanser.

Fill in the Blanks Fill in the bubble of the pair of words that best completes each sentence.

1. Every year a(n) _____ citizen of our town is awarded "_____ of the Community."

    (a.) upright, Rascal   (c.) sprightly, Bauble

    (b.) illustrious, Pillar   (d.) belligerent, Censor

NAME _____

2. Make sure the tightrope is _____ before you _____ out on it.
  a. notable, maneuver
  b. deflated, jaunt
  c. mediocre, pivot
  d. taut, venture

3. Even though the jury _____ him, he would always remain _____ to the villagers.
  a. idolized, nonchalant
  b. acquitted, notorious
  c. dispatched, sage
  d. censored, sprightly

4. My _____ and I find sharing ideas _____.
  a. baubles, fluted
  b. pillars, admissible
  c. colleagues, beneficial
  d. rascals, belligerent

5. Everyone agrees that Betsy's hard work on the project _____ a(n) _____ reward.
  a. deflates, fallow
  b. acquits, beneficial
  c. merits, tangible
  d. grieves, emotional

6. It's fun to _____ about ways to _____ a million dollars.
  a. isolate, disown
  b. maneuver, itemize
  c. decry, dispense
  d. speculate, squander

7. In the game of basketball, it is _____ to _____ with the ball, but not to walk with it.
  a. admissible, pivot
  b. beneficial, jaunt
  c. flippant, upkeep
  d. mediocre, dispatch

8. Your _____ attitude won't help solve our _____.
  a. notable, maneuver
  b. belligerent, dilemma
  c. external, elimination
  d. emotional, tenacity

9. The tropical fish will _____ in a tank filled with _____ water.
  a. maneuver, fallow
  b. grieve, sprightly
  c. flourish, saline
  d. venture, admissible

10. Lily should learn to _____ her _____ remarks before she speaks.
  a. censor, caustic
  b. acquit, fluted
  c. isolate, external
  d. itemize, flippant

73

Level H   Review 4–6

Classifying Words Sort the words in the box by writing each word to complete a phrase in the correct category.

accuracy	baubles	belligerent	colleague	defiance
dilute	dispensed	elimination	external	grudge
isolate	maneuver	nonchalant	pillar	platform
random	rung	tangible	upright	vacuum

Words You Might Use to Talk About Attitudes

1. trying to act calm and _____nonchalant_____ when you're really nervous
2. getting into fights because of his _____belligerent_____ attitude
3. looks like _____defiance_____ but really is shyness
4. bitter because she can't stop holding a(n) _____grudge_____
5. the _____upright_____ person who always tries to do the right thing

Words You Might Use to Talk About Ways to Earn Money

6. designing pretty _____baubles_____ to sell at craft fairs
7. offering to do _____random_____ chores for your neighbors
8. run the _____vacuum_____ cleaner and wash dishes
9. always more fun to work with a(n) _____colleague_____
10. proud when you've earned a(n) _____tangible_____ reward

Words You Might Use to Talk About Construction

11. paint or aluminum siding on the _____external_____ walls
12. _____maneuver_____ long boards around without knocking people down
13. a porch with a(n) _____pillar_____ on each side of the door
14. making sure each _____rung_____ of the ladder is unbroken and tight
15. beginning the deck by building a(n) _____platform_____

Words You Might Use to Talk About Science Experiments

16. figure out a way to _____isolate_____ each variable
17. recording results with perfect _____accuracy_____
18. water to _____dilute_____ a solution that is too strong
19. using chemicals only when _____dispensed_____ by your teacher
20. _____elimination_____ of a hypothesis you've proved incorrect

CHAPTER 7

WORD LIST

Read each word using the pronunciation key.

affect (ə fekt´)
benign (bi nīn´)
commencement (kə mens´ mənt)
dehydration (dē hī drā´ shən)
dimension (di men´ shən)
disposal (dis pō´ zəl)
endear (en dēr´)
falter (fôl´ tər)
forage (fôr´ ij)
harness (här´ nis)
immortality (im môr tal´ i tē)
jollity (jol´ i tē)
mete (mēt)
novelty (nov´ əl tē)
platoon (plə tōon´)
rebuttal (ri but´ əl)
savory (sā´ və rē)
squelch (skwelch)
torrent (tôr´ ent)
vertical (vər´ ti kəl)

WORD STUDY

Root Words

The Latin roots *spec*, and *spect* mean "to look" or "to look at."

expect (ek spekt´) *(v.)* 1. to look out for; 2. to anticipate

inspect (in spekt´) *(v.)* to look into or examine carefully

prospect (prä´ spekt) *(n.)* 1. something that is awaited or expected; 2. a possibility; 3. a vision

respect (ri spekt´) *(v.)* to honor or treat with esteem

spectacle (spek´ tə kəl) *(n.)* something held to public view

spectator (spek´ tā tər) *(n.)* someone who looks on or watches

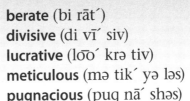

Challenge Words

berate (bi rāt´)
divisive (di vī´ siv)
lucrative (lōo´ krə tiv)
meticulous (mə tik´ yə ləs)
pugnacious (pug nā´ shəs)

Level H

■ **TEACHER TIP:** See page ix for suggestions on how to use this page.

WORDS IN CONTEXT

Read each sentence below to figure out the meaning of the word in **bold**. Use reasoning skills and the remainder of the sentence to help you. Write the meaning of the word on the line.

1. Some cities would like to **harness** the sun's power and convert it to electricity.

   <u>to bring under control</u>

2. What will **affect** your decision whether or not to try out for the soccer team?

   <u>to make something change</u>

3. The bus driver quickly **squelched** our noisy singing.

   <u>to stop</u>

4. The school is planning to hold the **commencement** activities outside.

   <u>a ceremony for graduation</u>

5. Newspaper **disposal** is easier with the new recycling program.

   <u>removal or destruction, especially of garbage</u>

6. The river rose in a **torrent** after last week's rain.

   <u>a raging flood</u>

7. **Savory** aromas drifted out of the cookie shop.

   <u>having a pleasant taste or smell</u>

8. The candidate's **rebuttal** to her opponent's remarks will appear in tomorrow's newspaper.

   <u>the offering of opposing evidence or arguments</u>

9. We wrote the room **dimensions** on paper so that we would know how much carpet to buy.

   <u>measures of length, width, or height</u>

10. During the winter months, all kinds of wildlife **forage** in our backyard.

    <u>to search for food</u>

WORD MEANINGS

Word Learning

Study the spelling, part(s) of speech, and meaning(s) of each word. Complete each sentence by writing the word on the line. Then read the sentence.

1. **affect** *(v.)* 1. to make something change; 2. to pretend

   The bad weather did not _____affect_____ his mood.

2. **benign** *(adj.)* gentle or harmless

   We found the mix-up to be a _____benign_____ mistake.

3. **commencement** *(n.)* 1. a beginning; 2. a ceremony for graduation

   She looked forward to the _____commencement_____ of the basketball season.

4. **dehydration** *(n.)* the removal or loss of water

   The apples shriveled and withered because of _____dehydration_____.

5. **dimension** *(n.)* a measure of length, width, or height

   Which _____dimension_____ of the box is too big?

6. **disposal** *(n.)* removal or getting rid of

   Our city treats waste _____disposal_____ as a serious issue.

7. **endear** *(v.)* to make dear or fond of

   Her whines and pleas did not _____endear_____ her to me.

8. **falter** *(v.)* 1. to hesitate; 2. to lapse in confidence; *(n.)* 1. unsure action; 2. quavering sound

   I will stand tall and never _____falter_____.

   I heard the _____falter_____ in his voice.

9. **forage** *(n.)* 1. food for animals; 2. a search for food or provisions; *(v.)* to search for food

   What do the birds do for winter _____forage_____?

   Hansel and Gretel had to _____forage_____ in the woods for their dinner.

10. **harness** *(n.)* the straps used on an animal to help it pull something; *(v.)* 1. to bring under control; 2. to utilize

    The horse struggled when placed in its _____harness_____.

    People use windmills to _____harness_____ the wind's power.

11. **immortality** *(n.)* 1. living forever; 2. lasting fame

    In Greek mythology, the gods sometimes granted _____immortality_____ to human beings.

12. **jollity** *(n.)* 1. a happy feeling; 2. merriment

    The singing and games created a tone of _____jollity_____ at the dinner table.

13. **mete** *(v.)* 1. to give out; 2. to distribute

    The council will _____mete_____ out a fitting punishment.

14. **novelty** *(n.)* 1. something new, unusual, or original; 2. newness

    My sister found the laughing duck quite a _____novelty_____.

15. **platoon** *(n.)* 1. division within a military company; 2. any group of people working together

    They belonged to the same _____platoon_____ when they were in the army.

16. **rebuttal** *(n.)* the offering of opposing evidence or arguments

    The professor offered no _____rebuttal_____ to my comment.

17. **savory** *(adj.)* having a pleasant taste or smell; *(n.)* one of a group of herbs used for cooking

    We ate a salad with a most _____savory_____ dressing.

    Did you put _____savory_____ in the soup?

18. **squelch** *(v.)* 1. to stop; 2. to put down with a remark; *(n.)* a harsh reply

    The strict measures tended to _____squelch_____ the workers' creativity.

    I could not ignore her stinging _____squelch_____ of my idea.

19. **torrent** *(n.)* 1. a raging flood; 2. any constant, strong flow

    A _____torrent_____ of shouts and cries greeted her as soon as she opened the window.

20. **vertical** *(adj.)* 1. lengthwise; 2. straight up and down or upright

    The _____vertical_____ length of the curtain exceeds that of the window.

Use Your Vocabulary

Choose the word from the Word List that best completes each sentence. Write the word on the line. You may use the plural form of nouns and the past tense of verbs if necessary.

Germany invaded Poland in 1939, marking the **1** of World War II. This invasion seriously **2** other nations. Led by Adolf Hitler, Germany invaded neighboring countries. People quickly realized that Hitler was anything but a(n) **3** influence in Europe. At first, the United States waited to see if other countries could **4** Hitler's aggressions. However, when Germany's ally, Japan, bombed Pearl Harbor, the United States entered the war and sent thousands of **5** abroad.

The war was difficult for the soldiers. Some marched through **6** of rain in jungle climates, while others suffered from **7** in the deserts. Officers tried to **8** out supplies fairly, but food was often scarce. At times, soldiers had to **9** and eat whatever food they could find. Many dreamed of the **10** meals they had enjoyed at home. Getting rest was difficult too. Some soldiers learned to sleep in a(n) **11** position so that they could be ready to move at any moment.

Famous entertainers would visit the army camps to bring soldiers a touch of laughter and **12** . The sight of people in civilian clothes was a(n) **13** and provided a boost to the soldiers' spirits.

Americans at home rarely **14** in their attempts to help the war effort. Many people worked in factories, planted gardens, rationed food, and managed the **15** and recycling of such materials as metal and rubber. Some women **16** themselves to soldiers by writing and sending news from home. Some soldiers gained **17** through their heroic deeds. Without the efforts of these soldiers, the war would have been lost.

After the war ended on May 8, 1945, negotiations for a peace treaty took place. Discussions about the new **18** of countries and territories often turned into disagreements. Finally, after a series of proposals and **19** , a treaty was written and signed. As part of the peace agreement, the United Nations was formed to help **20** any future aggression between nations.

1. _____ commencement
2. _____ affected
3. _____ benign
4. _____ harness
5. _____ platoons
6. _____ torrents
7. _____ dehydration
8. _____ mete
9. _____ forage
10. _____ savory
11. _____ vertical
12. _____ jollity
13. _____ novelty
14. _____ faltered
15. _____ disposal
16. _____ endeared
17. _____ immortality
18. _____ dimensions
19. _____ rebuttals
20. _____ squelch

79

SYNONYMS

Synonyms are words that have the same or nearly the same meanings.

Part 1 Choose the word from the box that is the best synonym for each group of words. Write the word on the line.

forage	**immortality**	**jollity**	**mete**
platoon	**rebuttal**	**squelch**	**torrent**

1. reply, retort, answer   rebuttal

2. feed; seek nourishment   forage

3. squad, company, outfit   platoon

4. eternal life, enduring celebrity   immortality

5. crush, suppress, silence   squelch

6. glee, gaiety   jollity

7. downpour, drenching, deluge   torrent

8. allot, hand out, dispense   mete

Part 2 Replace the underlined word with a word from the box that means the same or almost the same. Write your answer on the line.

affect	**dimensions**	**disposal**	**endear**
vertical	**novelty**	**benign**	

9. Emily is responsible for the <u>removal</u> of waste paper.   disposal

10. The new student managed to <u>charm</u> us with his playful antics.   endear

11. Did you measure the <u>proportions</u> of the old barn?   dimensions

12. We set the box down in an <u>upright</u> position.   vertical

13. Great amounts of stress can <u>influence</u> your health.   affect

14. After a while, the <u>newness</u> wore off. _____novelty_____

15. I'm sure she intended it as a <u>harmless</u> remark, so don't take offense.
_____benign_____

 **ANTONYMS**

Antonyms are words that have opposite or nearly opposite meanings.

Part 1 Choose the word from the box that is the best antonym for each group of words. Write the word on the line.

> dehydration   falter   harness   immortality   novelty

1. to let run wild _____harness_____

2. soaking, flooding, irrigation _____dehydration_____

3. something commonplace or everyday _____novelty_____

4. death, total obscurity _____immortality_____

5. go forward, stand strong; unsteady sound _____falter_____

Part 2 Replace the underlined word with a word from the box that means the opposite or almost the opposite. Write your answer on the line.

> jollity   squelch   jollity   benign   endear

6. They don't like to <u>promote</u> that kind of behavior. _____squelch_____

7. We dismissed a number of <u>harmful</u> suggestions. _____benign_____

8. Her little jokes <u>annoy</u> everyone in the family. _____endear_____

9. Her <u>misery</u> rubbed off on all of us. _____jollity_____

10. The sound of the gong marked the <u>completion</u> of the games.
_____commencement_____

WORD STUDY

Root Words Choose the word from the box that best completes each of the following sentences.

prospect	expect	inspect
respect	spectacle	spectator

1. Every _____spectator_____ cheered as the Olympic runner crossed the finish line.

2. I did not _____expect_____ such a warm welcome today.

3. You must _____respect_____ her wish to remain nameless.

4. The detective will carefully _____inspect_____ the scene of the crime.

5. The crowd gathered as the clown made a _____spectacle_____ of herself.

6. Troy was hopeful about the _____prospect_____ of a long vacation.

Vocabulary in Action

Can you think of a time when you were involved in a disagreement with a friend or family member? What was the most **divisive** issue you've had to contend with? How did it turn out? Were you able to persuade people to compromise?

Before he died on June 29, 1852, Henry Clay was famous for getting people, and even entire states, to compromise. Clay was born on a farm in Virginia in 1777. He became a U.S. representative, a senator, and the Secretary of State during the early 1800s, when tensions between the North and South threatened to split the Union. Henry Clay became known as "the Great Compromiser" when his skills maintained a balance between the free and the slave states. Clay helped draft three pieces of legislation that postponed the Civil War, including The Missouri Compromise and The Compromise of 1850.

In his famous speech on February 6, 1850, Clay argued for the preservation of the Union. Clay said, "I implore, as the best blessing which heaven can bestow upon me upon earth, that if the direful and sad event of the dissolution of the Union shall happen, I may not survive to behold the sad and heart-rending spectacle." His plea was granted when he died in 1852, nine years before the start of the Civil War.

CHALLENGE WORDS

Word Learning—Challenge!

Study the spelling, part of speech, and meaning(s) of each word. Complete each sentence by writing the word on the line. Then read the sentence.

1. **berate** *(v.)* to scold in a harsh way

   I know she'll _____**berate**_____ me for arriving late again.

2. **divisive** *(adj.)* 1. disruptive; 2. causing disagreement or division

   This is a _____**divisive**_____ issue, so I prefer not to discuss it.

3. **lucrative** *(adj.)* producing wealth; profitable

   Jody always has some _____**lucrative**_____ scheme in mind.

4. **meticulous** *(adj.)* 1. very careful about details; 2. fussy

   Christopher is extremely _____**meticulous**_____ about his homework.

5. **pugnacious** *(adj.)* eager to fight; combative

   A _____**pugnacious**_____ little bulldog lives in that yard.

Use Your Vocabulary—Challenge!

Project Care It's 1943. Jack and Gert know a number of soldiers in the war and decide to raise money to send care packages to all of the soldiers from their town. Write a story about their efforts to organize the people in the town for the fundraiser. Use the five Challenge Words above.

Vocabulary in Action

You can enjoy wordplay and expand your vocabulary by choosing a word and then making a list of all the words that can be made from it. In the Word Study box, you might choose the word ***expect*** and try to see how many variations of *expect* you can create:

Expect—expected, unexpected, unexpectedly, expecting, expectably, expectedness, expectant, expectancies, expectantly, expectations

Now choose a word from the Word Study box and see how many variations you can create. If you want to challenge yourself further, use each word in a sentence and identify its part of speech.

FUN WITH WORDS

Read the first pair of words on each line and think about the relationship between them. Write a word from the Word List in each blank to create a similar relationship between the second pair of words.

1. **herd** is to **cattle** as _____platoon_____ is to **soldiers**

2. **daylight** is to **dark** as **duplicate** is to _____novelty_____

3. **snow** is to **blizzard** as **rain** is to _____torrent_____

4. **upward** is to **downward** as **horizontal** is to _____vertical_____

5. **busy** is to **occupied** as **response** is to _____rebuttal_____

6. **registration** is to **enrollment** as **graduation** is to _____commencement_____

7. **build** is to **fire** as _____mete_____ is to **portions**

8. **practical** is to **impractical** as **mortality** is to _____immortality_____

9. **aunt** is to **relative** as **height** is to _____dimension_____

10. **peace** is to **war** as _____jollity_____ is to **despair**

Vocabulary in Action

The word *novelty* first appeared in English around 1382. It comes from the Old French word *novelté* ("newness") and the word *novel* ("new, strange, unusual"). The idea of a novelty as an object that is useless but amusing dates to around 1901. The phrase *novelty shop* first appeared around 1973.

WORD LIST

Read each word using the pronunciation key.

afflicted (ə flik´ tid)
bilk (bilk)
commend (kə mend´)
delicacy (del´ ə kə sē)
diminutive (di min´ yə tiv)
dissect (dī sekt´)
endeavor (en dev´ ər)
famine (fam´ in)
frail (frāl)
hectic (hek´ tik)
inadequate (in a´ də kwət)
kindle (kin´ dəl)
minimum (min´ ə məm)
obsolete (ob sə lēt´)
plausible (plô´ zə bəl)
receptacle (re cep´ tə kəl)
scrutinize (skrōō´ tə nīz)
stake (stāk)
torrid (tôr´ id)
vestige (ves´ tij)

WORD STUDY

Analogies

Analogies show relationships between pairs of words. Study the relationships between the pairs of words below.

rich is to **poor** as **tall** is to **short**

teacher is to **student** as **doctor** is to **patient**

heat is to **summer** as **cold** is to **winter**

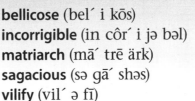

Challenge Words

bellicose (bel´ i kōs)
incorrigible (in côr´ i jə bəl)
matriarch (mā´ trē ärk)
sagacious (sə gā´ shəs)
vilify (vil´ ə fī)

■ **TEACHER TIP:** See page ix for suggestions on how to use this page.

WORDS IN CONTEXT

Read each sentence below to figure out the meaning of the word in **bold**. Use reasoning skills and the remainder of the sentence to help you. Write the meaning of the word on the line.

1. With the popularity of computers, typewriters have become **obsolete**.

   no longer in use

2. My grandmother is **afflicted** with arthritis, but she still likes to paint and to garden.

   suffering with

3. Jake's **hectic** band schedule includes four performances in a row.

   marked by feverish activity; hasty

4. If 30 hours is the maximum, what is the **minimum** number of hours you can volunteer each week?

   the least possible

5. People rushed to California in 1849 to **stake** a claim and pan for gold.

   to indicate boundaries with a stake; to assert a right or an ownership to something

6. The **frail** branches of the young tree did not fare well in the windstorm.

   easily broken

7. Due to the auditorium's inadequate **seating**, some of us had to stand.

   not enough; insufficient

8. The storybook character Thumbelina was able to sleep in a teacup because of her **diminutive** size.

   very small

9. Some people consider cooked flowers a **delicacy**.

   something pleasing to the senses

10. We'd better start to **kindle** the fire now because it may take a while.

    to start a fire

WORD MEANINGS

Word Learning

Study the spelling, part(s) of speech, and meaning(s) of each word. Complete each sentence by writing the word on the line. Then read the sentence.

1. **afflicted** *(adj.)* 1. suffering with; 2. troubled by

   My cousin is _____ aflicted _____ with the flu.

2. **bilk** *(v.)* 1. to cheat out of money; 2. to defraud; 3. to elude

   The police caught the man before he could _____ bilk _____ his creditors out of several thousand dollars.

3. **commend** *(v.)* 1. to praise; 2. to call attention to; 3. to recommend

   I _____ commend _____ your efforts to improve the situation.

4. **delicacy** *(n.)* 1. fragility; 2. softness; 3. something pleasing to the senses

   She admired the antique lace for its _____ delicacy _____.

5. **diminutive** *(adj.)* very small

   She wore a _____ diminutive _____ pocket watch on a chain.

6. **dissect** *(v.)* 1. to cut apart or separate; 2. to examine

   I can't wait to _____ dissect _____ worms in biology class!

7. **endeavor** *(n.)* a good try or attempt; *(v.)* to try or strive

   To build your own log cabin is an ambitious _____ endeavor _____.

   And now, we will _____ endeavor _____ to study for the final exam.

8. **famine** *(n.)* 1. a serious shortage of food; 2. starvation

   My ancestors came here from Ireland during the potato _____ famine _____.

9. **frail** *(adj.)* 1. not strong or hearty; weak; 2. easily broken

   Mrs. Rulas was _____ frail _____ after a major operation.

10. **hectic** *(adj.)* marked by feverish activity; hasty

    It's been a _____ hectic _____ day, and we're very tired.

11. **inadequate** *(adj.)* 1. not enough; insufficient; 2. not able

    His _____ inadequate _____ efforts to fix the faucet resulted in a huge flood.

12. **kindle** *(v.)* 1. to start a fire; 2. to set in action; 3. to inspire

To our alarm, we saw lightning _____kindle_____ a fire in the backyard.

13. **minimum** *(n.)* the smallest amount possible; *(adj.)* the least possible

We need a _____minimum_____ of four dollars.

What is the _____minimum_____ skill level among the gymnasts on your team?

14. **obsolete** *(adj.)* 1. no longer in use; 2. out-of-date

That garage doesn't sell any _____obsolete_____ auto parts.

15. **plausible** *(adj.)* 1. likely; 2. acceptable; 3. apparently believable

His explanation seems _____plausible_____ to me.

16. **receptacle** *(n.)* something that holds or contains; a container

Will you throw those apple cores in the trash _____receptacle_____?

17. **scrutinize** *(v.)* 1. to watch carefully; 2. to examine

I will be sure to _____scrutinize_____ these papers before I sign them.

18. **stake** *(n.)* a sharpened wood or metal piece hammered into the ground as a marker or support; *(v.)* 1. to indicate boundaries with a stake; 2. to assert a right or an ownership to something

Tie the bottom of the tent to this _____stake_____.

Anyone can come and _____stake_____ out a territory.

19. **torrid** *(adj.)* 1. dried by the sun's heat; 2. burning

Camels are well adapted to walking on the desert's _____torrid_____ sands.

20. **vestige** *(n.)* a mark or trace of something no longer present

Mary searched the house for some _____vestige_____ of the previous owners.

Notable Quotes

"I say in speeches that a **plausible** mission of artists is to make people appreciate being alive at least a little bit. I am then asked if I know of any artists who pulled that off. I reply, 'The Beatles did.'"

—Kurt Vonnegut (1922–2007), author (from *Timequake*)

Use Your Vocabulary

Choose the word from the Word List that best completes each sentence. Write the word on the line. You may use the plural form of nouns and the past tense of verbs if necessary.

When my parents were younger, they joined an organization of volunteers who __1__ to assist people in developing countries. My parents went to a country in Africa that was suffering from drought and __2__. They went to a village where the crops were __3__ with insects.

At first, the villagers did not trust my parents and feared that the strangers had come to __4__ them out of what little they had. They __5__ my parents' behavior for several weeks before they would listen to their ideas. Finally, Abraha, the leader of the village, sat down to talk with my parents. He found their ideas __6__, but said they needed to learn more about the plants, animals, and soil in this environment.

My parents were accustomed to a(n) __7__ pace of life, but the villagers did things more slowly. Abraha showed them __8__, green plants growing out of the soil. At this stage, they were still healthy, but their __9__ made them vulnerable to insects. The __10__ creatures presented a great threat. Abraha and my mother __11__ seeds to examine them for insects, while my father helped the farmers __12__ out the __13__ fields.

The village had suffered __14__ rainfall for several years and had nearly __15__ farming equipment— __16__ of long ago. But they did very well with the tools that they had and built large __17__ called cisterns to collect and store the rain that did fall. They hoped that they would get at least the __18__ amount of necessary rain.

At harvest time, everyone realized that their work had paid off and that luck had provided them with sufficient rain as well. The crops had yielded enough food to eat, and there would even be enough to sell to others. They __19__ one another for their hard work. The successful cooperation __20__ a friendship that my parents and the villagers maintain today.

1. _____ endeavor
2. _____ famine
3. _____ afflicted
4. _____ bilk
5. _____ scrutinized
6. _____ plausible
7. _____ hectic
8. _____ frail
9. _____ delicacy
10. _____ diminutive
11. _____ dissected
12. _____ stake
13. _____ torrid
14. _____ inadequate
15. _____ obsolete
16. _____ vestiges
17. _____ receptacles
18. _____ minimum
19. _____ commended
20. _____ kindled

SYNONYMS

Synonyms are words that have the same or nearly the same meanings.

Part 1 Choose the word from the box that is the best synonym for each group of words. Write the word on the line.

scrutinize	bilk	commend	inadequate
diminutive	obsolete	afflicted	torrid

1. tiny, miniature, little _____ diminutive

2. plagued, burdened with _____ afflicted

3. scorching, parched _____ torrid

4. swindle, con, deceive _____ bilk

5. compliment, extol, support _____ commend

6. deficient, lacking, incomplete _____ inadequate

7. defunct, bygone, extinct _____ obsolete

8. study, consider, ponder _____ scrutinize

Part 2 Replace the underlined word with a word from the box that means the same or almost the same. Write your answer on the line.

kindle	plausible	hectic	receptacle
vestige	frail	endeavor	

9. There's a <u>bucket</u> for the leftover rags in the corner. _____ receptacle

10. The week continued at a <u>frenzied</u> pace. _____ hectic

11. The calligraphy exhibit might <u>arouse</u> your interest. _____ kindle

12. She offered no <u>convincing</u> argument for spending so much money.
_____ plausible

13. After such a noble <u>effort</u>, I think you will succeed. _____ endeavor

14. That old hitching post is a <u>remnant</u> of the horse-and-buggy days.

_____vestige_____

15. I'm afraid the bird will break its <u>fragile</u> bones if it flies into the window.

_____frail_____

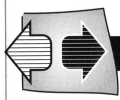 **ANTONYMS**

Antonyms are words that have opposite or nearly opposite meanings.

Part 1 Choose the word from the box that is the best antonym for each group of words. Write the word on the line.

afflicted	commend	diminutive
hectic	torrid	plausible

1. enormous, gigantic, massive _____diminutive_____

2. slow paced; relaxed _____hectic_____

3. blame, disapprove, protest _____commend_____

4. comfortable, healthy, at ease _____afflicted_____

5. doubtful, questionable, improbable _____plausible_____

6. frosty, freezing, icy _____torrid_____

Part 2 Replace the underlined word with a word from the box that means the opposite or almost the opposite. Write your answer on the line.

famine	inadequate	frail
obsolete	kindle	minimum

7. Katie set the stereo at the <u>maximum</u> volume level. _____minimum_____

8. He made a few <u>powerful</u> attempts to move the boulder, but it wouldn't budge.

_____frail_____

9. My aunt always tried to <u>smother</u> my interest in theater. _____kindle_____

10. After the war, the country enjoyed a time of <u>abundance</u>. _____famine_____

91

11. The company has a warehouse full of <u>modern</u> equipment. <u>   obsolete   </u>

12. We have <u>sufficient</u> room to move around. <u>   inadequate   </u>

WORD STUDY

Analogies To complete the following analogies, decide what kind of relationship is shown by the first pair of words. Then fill in the bubble next to the other pair of words that shows the same relationship.

1. expose is to **secret** as
- **a.** unwrap is to gift
- **b.** shovel is to snow
- **c.** write is to table
- **d.** eat is to food

2. drizzle is to **rain** as
- **a.** remember is to tell
- **b.** giggle is to snicker
- **c.** nibble is to eat
- **d.** hate is to love

3. caboose is to **train** as
- **a.** hat is to hair
- **b.** dog is to house
- **c.** glass is to water
- **d.** suffix is to word

4. accountant is to **spreadsheets** as
- **a.** teacher is to student
- **b.** barber is to scissors
- **c.** firefighter is to fire
- **d.** president is to people

5. moderate is to **extreme** as
- **a.** soft is to loud
- **b.** blue is to proud
- **c.** rainy is to cloudy
- **d.** popular is to lovely

6. portrait is to **painting** as
- **a.** clay is to pot
- **b.** pen is to pencil
- **c.** monument is to sculpture
- **d.** carrot is to garden

CHALLENGE WORDS

Word Learning—Challenge!

Study the spelling, part of speech, and meaning of each word. Complete each sentence by writing the word on the line. Then read the sentence.

1. **bellicose** *(adj.)* eager to start wars or quarrels

   We have as little contact as possible with that _____ bellicose _____ group next door.

2. **incorrigible** *(adj.)* unmanageable or unable to be improved

   I won't babysit for them because their little girl is _____ incorrigible _____.

3. **matriarch** *(n.)* a female who dominates a family or group

   I've never seen a _____ matriarch _____ like my Aunt Margaret.

4. **sagacious** *(adj.)* having good judgment or keen perception

   Josh relied on the _____ sagacious _____ advice of his older brother.

5. **vilify** *(v.)* to make rude or vicious statements against

   The journalist made up false reports to _____ vilify _____ the city council members.

Use Your Vocabulary—Challenge!

Summer Daze It's a dry summer in your community, and no one's garden is growing. Neighbors are starting to fight over the use of water. On a separate sheet of paper, use the Challenge Words above to write a story about the water shortage and what people do about it. Be creative!

> ### Vocabulary in Action
>
> The word **matriarch** is a combination of two Latin roots. It contains the root *matr*, which means "mother," and *arch*, which means "chief." When you combine these two roots, you arrive at the definition of matriarch, a female who dominates a family or group, in other words, a chief mother.

Twelve vocabulary words are hidden in the puzzle below. Find each word and circle it.
Words may be forward, backward, up, down, or diagonal.

```
A M I N T R E V Y L A N F P X I
R F A T H I A Q R H E C T A R S
T I F S T A M U M I N I M R E C
O B S L E R I A A C Y T I G Q R
E A R O I B N K M O V E C T E U
K I N O N C X M E M Q U A C E T
A L L R E R T D I M I N V E M I
T R U C W A N E B E N D E S L N
S T A R J N O L D N I H M S K I
F B R H B I L I J D T X Q I Y Z
R U T I N N X C K A I L N D R E
A T L R Y I R A E R K D T J O K
I K O S T Z K C L P L T I G E R
L A H B R C A Y P E T R O B S O
O Y T A L E L B I S U A L P I B
T O R R I D S T J A G U Q T E R
```

Vocabulary in Action

Before the word **bilk** meant "to defraud," it was a term
from the game of cribbage. In cribbage, a bilk happens
when a player stops an opponent by spoiling his score.
Though no one knows for sure where the word comes
from, some scholars believe it is from an Arab word
that means "a word signifying nothing." Others think
it may be a variation on the word *balk*.

WORD LIST

Read each word using the pronunciation key.

affinity (ə fin′ ə tē)
blanch (blanch)
component (kəm pō′ nənt)
descend (di send′)
diplomat (dip′ lə mat)
diverse (də vərs′)
endorse (en dôrs′)
fantasy (fan′ tə sē)
frequency (frē′ kwən sē)
hedge (hej)
incise (in sīz′)
knoll (nōl)
monarchy (mon′ är kē)
opaque (ō pāk′)
plunder (plun′ dər)
recess (rē′ ses)
secrete (sə krēt′)
stammer (stam′ ər)
tranquil (traŋ′ kwəl)
voluble (vol′ yə bəl)

WORD STUDY

Suffixes

The suffix *-less* means "without, not able to," or "not able to be."

countless (kount′ ləs) *(adj.)* unable to be counted

helpless (help′ ləs) *(adj.)* without help; not able to help oneself

hopeless (hōp′ ləs) *(adj.)* without hope

sleepless (slēp′ ləs) *(adj.)* without sleep; unable to sleep

stainless (stān′ ləs) *(adj.)* without stains; unable to be stained

worthless (wərth′ ləs) *(adj.)* without worth or value

Challenge Words

fabricate (fab′ ri kāt)
innovate (in′ ə vāt)
retrospect (re′ trə spekt)
supplant (sə plant′)
tenacious (tə nā′ shəs)

■ **TEACHER TIP:** See page ix for suggestions on how to use this page.

Read each sentence below to figure out the meaning of the word in **bold**. Use reasoning skills and the remainder of the sentence to help you. Write the meaning of the word on the line.

1. Always the **diplomat**, Irene calmed her brothers and settled their argument.

someone skilled in talking effectively with people

2. Judge Harris told the jury to take a 15-minute **recess**.

a pause in an activity

3. The mayoral candidate hoped that the city newspaper would **endorse** him.

to write one's name on a document to show approval

4. After Ben threw the water balloon, I chased him over the **hedge**.

a row of bushes

5. I need boiling water to **blanch** the vegetables before adding them to the sauce.

to boil briefly

6. Tiffany seems to have a natural **affinity** for baseball.

a natural liking for or an attraction to someone or something

7. What are the chemical **components** of water?

a part; element; ingredient

8. Ryan was engrossed in a conversation with our **voluble** neighbor.

speaking with a steady flow of words; talkative

9. The noisy children quickly disturbed the park's **tranquil** atmosphere.

calm

10. We didn't want anyone to see into the garage, so we covered the windows with an **opaque** layer of paint.

unable to be penetrated by light

WORD MEANINGS

Word Learning

Study the spelling, part(s) of speech, and meaning(s) of each word. Complete each sentence by writing the word on the line. Then read the sentence.

1. **affinity** *(n.)* a natural liking for or an attraction to someone or something

    The two have a real _____ affinity _____ for each other.

2. **blanch** *(v.)* 1. to take the color from; 2. to whiten; 3. to boil briefly

    I'm afraid the sun will _____ blanch _____ these curtains if we let them hang out to dry.

3. **component** *(n.)* a part; element; ingredient

    Sunlight is a critical _____ component _____ of photosynthesis.

4. **descend** *(v.)* to move from a higher place to a lower place

    We sat on the beach at dusk and watched the sun _____ descend _____ and seem to melt into the horizon.

5. **diplomat** *(n.)* 1. one who represents a government in dealing with other governments; 2. someone skilled in talking effectively with people

    If you want to become a _____ diplomat _____, you should learn at least one foreign language.

6. **diverse** *(adj.)* 1. different; 2. having variety

    The United Nations represents many _____ diverse _____ cultures.

7. **endorse** *(v.)* 1. to write one's name on a document to show approval; 2. to approve

    I wanted to do my homework in front of the TV, but my father did not _____ endorse _____ the idea.

8. **fantasy** *(n.)* 1. imagination; a product of the mind; 2. a foolish notion

    She traveled to Hollywood and fulfilled her _____ fantasy _____ of becoming an actress.

9. **frequency** *(n.)* 1. how often something happens; 2. number of repetitions of an electrical current

    The _____ frequency _____ of thunderstorms always increases in summer.

10. **hedge** *(n.)* a row of bushes; *(v.)* 1. to confine; 2. to avoid

    Don't _____ hedge _____ the question by trying to divert my attention.

11. **incise** *(v.)* to cut into

She decided to _____ incise _____ her initials into the bench.

12. **knoll** *(n.)* a rounded hill or mound

The coyote stood on the grassy _____ knoll _____ and howled at the rising moon.

13. **monarchy** *(n.)* a government under one leader, such as a king, a queen, or an emperor, usually determined by birth

The French revolutionaries fought for an end to the _____ monarchy _____.

14. **opaque** *(adj.)* unable to be penetrated by light

An _____ opaque _____ shade hangs in front of the window.

15. **plunder** *(v.)* to rob by open force, as in war; *(n.)* 1. robbery by open force; 2. anything taken by robbery

During the war, soldiers would _____ plunder _____ small villages.

Afterwards, they were forced by treaty to return their _____ plunder _____.

16. **recess** *(n.)* 1. a pause in an activity; 2. a small hollow

We spoke briefly during the _____ recess _____.

17. **secrete** *(v.)* 1. to give off fluids or other cells from a living body; 2. to hide something away in secret

Animals recognize other animals by oils and scents that they _____ secrete _____.

18. **stammer** *(v.)* to make involuntary interruptions in speech

She tried not to _____ stammer _____ during her oral report.

19. **tranquil** *(adj.)* 1. free from problems; 2. calm; 3. still

My old friends live in a _____ tranquil _____ village in the mountains.

20. **voluble** *(adj.)* speaking with a steady flow of words; talkative

With my _____ voluble _____ companion, I couldn't get a word in edgewise.

> ## *Vocabulary in Action*
>
> The word ***fantasy*** first appeared in English around 1325 and comes from the Latin *phantasia*, meaning "appearance, image, perception, imagination." People first began to think of a fantasy as a "daydream based on desires" around 1926.

Use Your Vocabulary

Choose the word from the Word List that best completes each sentence. Write the word on the line. You may use the plural form of nouns and the past tense of verbs if necessary.

Maggie lived in a house in the __1__ of a hill. She liked living in the __2__ wilderness, but __3__ the hill into town with some __4__. Every week she would stand on the grassy __5__, look down at the town, and say, "Littleville, here I come!"

Everyone in Littleville knew it when Maggie came to visit. She was quite __6__, and she had a(n) __7__ for foreign languages. Littleville lay on the border of Biggaly and Middley. Many Biggalians and Middlers came to Littleville to live. Maggie enjoyed practicing her languages with the town's __8__ inhabitants. Littleville's Queen Isabel disliked all Biggalians. She felt they wanted to overthrow her __9__.

One day Maggie arrived in Littleville to find a commotion in the town square. She asked her friend Ivan what was going on.

"Oh, it's terrible," Ivan said. "That horrible mob from Biggaly broke into Judge Lucas's cellar and stole his jewels! The thieves have been captured, but it seems they have __10__ away their __11__."

Maggie looked confused. "How did they know his jewels were there? He has __12__ windows and a thorny __13__ around his house. There are several __14__ to this story that I don't understand."

Before Ivan could answer, Queen Isabel stood in front of Lucas's house and called for quiet. Matthias, the Biggalian __15__, stepped forward.

"Isabel," said Matthias, "I cannot __16__ the arrest of my fellow Biggalians. They did not steal Lucas's jewels."

"That's pure __17__!" Isabel said. "You know they did. " She turned around, and a thorn from the hedge __18__ a hole in the cloth bag she wore at her belt. Jewels tumbled from the sack.

"Those are my jewels!" Lucas cried. "Isabel, you stole them!" Isabel's face __19__, and she __20__, "I—I—I can explain!" But the police came to arrest her before she had the chance.

1. _____ recess
2. _____ tranquil
3. _____ descended
4. _____ frequency
5. _____ knoll
6. _____ voluble
7. _____ affinity
8. _____ diverse
9. _____ monarchy
10. _____ secreted
11. _____ plunder
12. _____ opaque
13. _____ hedge
14. _____ components
15. _____ diplomat
16. _____ endorse
17. _____ fantasy
18. _____ incised
19. _____ blanched
20. _____ stammered

SYNONYMS

Synonyms are words that have the same or nearly the same meanings.

Part 1 Choose the word from the box that is the best synonym for each group of words. Write the word on the line.

affinity	component	endorse	opaque
plunder	recess	secrete	voluble

1. subscribe to, support, ratify _____ endorse

2. fondness for, appeal _____ affinity

3. chatty, long-winded _____ voluble

4. loot, ransack; spoils _____ plunder

5. piece, segment, factor _____ component

6. issue, discharge, conceal _____ secrete

7. not transparent, obscure _____ opaque

8. break, pause, niche _____ recess

Part 2 Replace the underlined word(s) with a word from the box that means the same or almost the same. Write your answer on the line.

descend	diverse	fantasy	hedge
knoll	stammer	tranquil	

9. Lacy sat on the <u>hill</u> in the backyard and watched the clouds.
_____ knoll

10. Sue sat down to enjoy the <u>peaceful</u> afternoon. _____ tranquil

11. In awe, we watched the princess <u>come down</u> the staircase. _____ descend

12. If you go into that bakery, you will find a <u>varied</u> assortment of cakes, cookies, and breads. _____ diverse

13. When asked to respond to the charges, he could only <u>stutter</u> his reply.
_____ stammer

14. Why does he keep trying to <u>dodge</u> the issue? _____hedge_____

15. Dara was surprised when her mother told her that the tales of the Easter Bunny are all <u>make-believe</u>. _____fantasy_____

ANTONYMS

Antonyms are words that have opposite or nearly opposite meanings.

Part 1 Choose the word from the box that is the best antonym for each group of words. Write the word on the line.

fantasy	blanch	affinity	frequency	diverse

1. rejection, aversion, dislike _____affinity_____

2. identical, alike, same _____diverse_____

3. reality, actuality, truth _____fantasy_____

4. rarity, uncommonness _____frequency_____

5. dye, brighten _____blanch_____

Part 2 Replace the underlined word with a word from the box that means the opposite or almost the opposite. Write your answer on the line.

descends	endorses	opaque	tranquil	voluble

6. Did you talk to that <u>quiet</u> woman in the blue hat? _____voluble_____

7. I looked into her <u>troubled</u> face. _____tranquil_____

8. Each morning the spider <u>ascends</u> the doorway and crawls into her web.
_____descends_____

9. He wore a <u>clear</u> green stone pinned to his cape. _____opaque_____

10. Nick <u>disputes</u> the idea, but he is too shy to speak up. _____endorses_____

WORD STUDY

Suffixes Choose the adjective that best describes each of the following people, objects, or events.

countless	hopeless	helpless
sleepless	stainless	worthless

1. a newborn baby   helpless

2. a long night   sleepless

3. blades of grass   countless

4. a steel pan   stainless

5. a piece of junk   worthless

6. a situation   hopeless

Vocabulary in Action

Are you interested in science and scientific experiments? Maybe you could be the next Elwood Haynes. You may not have heard of Haynes, but you may be familiar with some of his inventions: **stainless** steel, the thermostat, and the horseless carriage. Born in Portland, Indiana, on October 14, 1857, Haynes invented one of the first successful gasoline-powered automobiles. He also invented the thermostat used in houses and many other items. As a young boy, Haynes was curious about how things worked. When he was 12 he read his sister's college chemistry book, and by 15 he was experimenting with metallic substances made of two or more elements. In 1886, natural gas was found in Haynes's hometown. After this discovery, he organized a company to supply it to the town.

CHALLENGE WORDS

Word Learning—Challenge!

Study the spelling, part of speech, and meaning(s) of each word. Complete each sentence by writing the word on the line. Then read the sentence.

1. **fabricate** *(v.)* 1. to make up; 2. to invent

   If you ask him and he doesn't know, he'll _____fabricate_____ an answer.

2. **innovate** *(v.)* to develop a new way of doing something

   Necessity often forces people to _____innovate_____.

3. **retrospect** *(n.)* the act of thinking about the past or looking back

   In _____retrospect_____, I'd say we could have done things differently.

4. **supplant** *(v.)* to take the place of, especially through force or trickery

   The knight thought about his scheme to _____supplant_____ the monarch.

5. **tenacious** *(adj.)* 1. holding firmly or tightly; 2. persistent or stubborn

   You can try to change her mind, but she is really _____tenacious_____.

Use Your Vocabulary—Challenge!

The Plot Thickens You have discovered a plot to overturn the government of Middley, which is near Littleville and Biggaly. Use the five Challenge Words above to write a story about the schemers and their plans. Are they successful? You decide!

Vocabulary in Action

"The memory should be specially taxed in youth, since it is then that it is strongest and most **tenacious.** But in choosing the things that should be committed to memory, the utmost care and forethought must be exercised; as lessons well-learned in youth are never forgotten."

—Arthur Schopenhauer (1788–1860), German philosopher

Start your own story notebook. On the lines below, make a list of story ideas. Use at least 10 chapter vocabulary words from this chapter in your list.

Answers will vary.

Review 7–9

Word Meanings Fill in the bubble of the word that is best defined by each phrase.

1. a fast flow of water
   - (a.) famine
   - (b.) knoll
   - (c.) torrent
   - (d.) vestige

2. scorching or fiery
   - **(a.) torrid**
   - (b.) savory
   - (c.) diminutive
   - (d.) opaque

3. not the same
   - (a.) benign
   - (b.) tranquil
   - (c.) obsolete
   - (d.) diverse

4. to speak in a halting manner
   - **(a.) stammer**
   - (b.) plunder
   - (c.) secrete
   - (d.) blanch

5. happening at a frantic pace
   - (a.) tranquil
   - **(b.) hectic**
   - (c.) vertical
   - (d.) inadequate

6. one piece of something
   - (a.) rebuttal
   - (b.) novelty
   - **(c.) component**
   - (d.) fantasy

7. seemingly possible or believable
   - (a.) afflicted
   - (b.) voluble
   - (c.) frail
   - **(d.) plausible**

8. to measure out
   - **(a.) mete**
   - (b.) kindle
   - (c.) harness
   - (d.) descend

9. to study with care
   - (a.) falter
   - **(b.) scrutinize**
   - (c.) incise
   - (d.) stake

10. to point out as deserving of praise
    - (a.) squelch
    - (b.) hedge
    - **(c.) commend**
    - (d.) endear

11. to swindle or trick
    - (a.) incise
    - (b.) dissect
    - **(c.) bilk**
    - (d.) stammer

12. to show support for or acceptance of
    - **(a.) endorse**
    - (b.) mete
    - (c.) falter
    - (d.) forage

13. a good effort
    - (a.) dehydration
    - (b.) immortality
    - **(c.) endeavor**
    - (d.) frequency

14. a fondness for someone or something
    - (a.) recess
    - **(b.) affinity**
    - (c.) dimension
    - (d.) receptacle

15. a person who is a skilled negotiator
    - (a.) platoon
    - **(b.) diplomat**
    - (c.) monarchy
    - (d.) commencement

16. a state of merriment
    - **(a.) jollity**
    - (b.) torrent
    - (c.) minimum
    - (d.) component

17. not allowing light to pass through

    a. opaque   **b.** vertical   **c.** torrid   **d.** hectic

18. showing kindness

    a. frail   **b.** voluble   **c.** benign   **d.** plausible

19. anything stolen

    a. knoll   **b.** plunder   **c.** disposal   **d.** novelty

20. to move downward

    a. affect   **b.** endear   **c.** scrutinize   **d.** descend

Sentence Completion Choose the word from the box that best completes each of the following sentences. Write the word in the blank.

| fantasy | platoon | secrete | dehydration | obsolete |
| dimensions | savory | rebuttal | inadequate | commencement |

1. We had a(n) _____savory_____ meal at that famous restaurant.

2. Todd gave us _____inadequate_____ directions, but we still made it.

3. Do you know the _____dimensions_____ of your new room?

4. My sister's _____platoon_____ is stationed overseas.

5. Digital music has made records nearly _____obsolete_____.

6. At one time, the idea of space travel was nothing more than a(n) _____fantasy_____.

7. June 1 marks the _____commencement_____ of our summer vacation.

8. The thief decided to _____secrete_____ the stolen silver, but before he had a chance to do, it he was caught.

9. Take plenty of water on your hike to protect against _____dehydration_____.

10. Each debater has three minutes for _____rebuttal_____.

Fill in the Blanks Fill in the bubble of the pair of words that best completes each sentence.

1. Our teacher said that to _____ a frog, you must _____ its chest cavity.

    a. endorse, harness   **c.** commend, scrutinize

    b. dissect, incise   **d.** blanch, falter

2. Each pirate tried to _____ the others out of their share of the _____.

  a. hedge, jollity   **c.** bilk, plunder

  b. mete, receptacle   **d.** squelch, vestige

3. The tiny pony wears a(n) _____ _____ in the show ring.

  a. savory delicacy   **c.** opaque receptacle

  b. diminutive harness   **d.** frail stake

4. The students will _____ to work with the _____ computers until the new ones arrive.

  a. endorse, inadequate   **c.** endeavor, obsolete

  b. descend, hectic   **d.** falter, afflicted

5. An important _____ gave the _____ speech.

  a. dimension, plausible   **c.** platoon, rebuttal

  b. diplomat, commencement   **d.** delicacy, tranquil

6. When the _____ meal was finished, there was not one _____ of food left over.

  a. torrid, torrent   **c.** hectic, disposal

  b. vertical, famine   **d.** savory, vestige

7. My best friend and I share a(n) _____ for books about the British _____.

  a. affinity, monarchy   **c.** immortality, torrent

  b. receptacle, dimension   **d.** commencement, famine

8. The _____ child _____ himself to his uncle by saying "I love you" over and over again.

  a. diverse, kindled   **c.** voluble, endeared

  b. tranquil, descended   **d.** plausible, commended

9. Dean has a recurring _____ about being the leader of a military _____.

  a. component, dehydration   **c.** minimum, monarchy

  b. rebuttal, stake   **d.** fantasy, platoon

10. A _____ of water rushed down the almost _____ face of the cliff.

  a. dehydration, afflicted   **c.** recess, tranquil

  b. torrent, vertical   **d.** vestige, frail

Classifying Words

Sort the words in the box by writing each word to complete a phrase in the correct category.

benign	blanched	commencement	components	delicacy
diminutive	diplomat	diverse	endeavor	forage
frail	inadequate	immortality	jollity	monarchy
platoon	plausible	recess	savory	scrutinize

Words You Might Use to Talk About Food

1. likes raw vegetables better than _____blanched_____ ones
2. looking forward to a(n) _____savory_____ dessert
3. several _____components_____ of a good meal
4. consider fish eggs a rare _____delicacy_____
5. not have to _____forage_____ for food

Words You Might Use to Talk About How People Look

6. pale little boy who is thin and _____frail_____
7. an expression of _____jollity_____ in her twinkling eyes
8. a tall friend and another friend who is _____diminutive_____
9. _____scrutinize_____ us with those piercing blue eyes
10. a _____benign_____ smile on her friendly face

Words You Might Use to Talk About Careers

11. to join a(n) _____platoon_____ of soldiers
12. _____inadequate_____ grades for becoming a doctor
13. exciting career as a(n) _____diplomat_____ in the foreign service
14. need to be born to a career in a(n) _____monarchy_____
15. great painters who have achieved _____immortality_____

Words You Might Use to Talk About Education

16. strange that your school career ends with _____commencement_____
17. spending time with your friends during _____recess_____
18. _____endeavor_____ to learn as much as you can
19. thinking of a(n) _____plausible_____ excuse for forgetting your homework
20. a _____diverse_____ range of classes in high school and college

WORD LIST

Read each word using the pronunciation key.

agitate (aj´ ə tāt)
bounteous (boun´ tē əs)
comprise (kəm prīz´)
despondent (di spän´ dənt)
disassociate (dis ə sō´ sē āt)
dominant (däm´ ə nənt)
engaged (in gājd´)
fatigue (fə tēg´)
fugitive (fyōō´ jə tiv)
hesitant (hez´ ə tənt)
indifferent (in dif´ rənt)
laborious (lə bôr´ ē əs)
monopoly (mə näp´ ə lē)
optical (äp´ ti kəl)
portray (pôr trā´)
recluse (rek´ lōōs)
sedate (si dāt´)
static (stat´ ik)
transact (tran zakt´)
wane (wān)

WORD STUDY

Root Words

The Greek root *log* means "the study of" or "word."

dialogue (dī´ ə lôg) *(n.)* a conversation; an exchange of ideas
eulogy (yōō´ lə gē) *(n.)* an oral or a written tribute to a person who has died
logistics (lō jis´ tiks) *(n.)* the planning and managing of an undertaking
monologue (mon´ ə lôg) *(n.)* a long speech by one person
technology (tek nol´ ə jē) *(n.)* use of scientific knowledge to solve problems and control physical forces
zoology (zōō lə´ jē) *(n.)* the study of animals

Challenge Words

arbitrary (är´ bə trâr ē)
conspicuous (kən spik´ yōō əs)
envisage (en vis´ əj)
lackadaisical (lak ə dāz´ i kəl)
optimum (op tə´ məm)

Level H

■ **TEACHER TIP:** See page ix for suggestions on how to use this page.

WORDS IN CONTEXT

Read each sentence below to figure out the meaning of the word in **bold**. Use reasoning skills and the remainder of the sentence to help you. Write the meaning of the word on the line.

1. You won't get any suggestions from her; she's **indifferent** on the matter.

> having no feeling about or opinion of

2. When cold weather comes, my interest in swimming tends to **wane**.

> to gradually decrease in size or amount

3. A washing machine **agitates** clothes in soapy water to clean them.

> to shake or stir

4. Josh was **engaged** in a discussion with a customer, so we didn't bother him.

> busy or occupied

5. According to legend, an old **recluse** has lived in that cave for 50 years.

> someone who lives apart from society

6. Beth will **portray** Helen Keller in our school production of *The Miracle Worker*.

> to act out onstage

7. Javier appeared **hesitant** to join the soccer team, but he decided to in the end.

> holding back; not able to decide

8. Who has the **dominant** influence in this group?

> ruling or controlling

9. Our **bounteous** garden produced flowers of all sizes and colors.

> giving generously

10. I always hear too much **static** on my portable radio.

> interference with radio or television reception due to electric disturbance

WORD MEANINGS

Word Learning

Study the spelling, part(s) of speech, and meaning(s) of each word. Complete each sentence by writing the word on the line. Then read the sentence.

1. **agitate** *(v.)* 1. to shake or stir; 2. to upset or excite emotionally

   I didn't want to _____agitate_____ the situation, so I said nothing.

2. **bounteous** *(adj.)* 1. giving generously; 2. ample or plentiful

   We sat down to a _____bounteous_____ feast.

3. **comprise** *(v.)* 1. to include or contain; 2. to make up

   This is one of the four verses that _____compromise_____ the song.

4. **despondent** *(adj.)* 1. feeling sad or discouraged; 2. wanting to give up

   Jessie lost her job, so she's feeling rather _____despondent_____.

5. **disassociate** *(v.)* to end contact with someone or something

   I think that after all this trouble, she'll probably _____disassociate_____ herself from that group.

6. **dominant** *(adj.)* 1. ruling or controlling; 2. foremost

   Over there you can see the _____dominant_____ wolf in the pack.

7. **engaged** *(adj.)* 1. busy or occupied; 2. planning to be married

   Can Harry come with us on Friday, or is he otherwise _____engaged_____?

8. **fatigue** *(n.)* 1. weariness; 2. mental or physical exhaustion; *(v.)* to tire out

   He went to the doctor complaining of _____fatigue_____ and headaches.

   Reading without sufficient light will _____fatigue_____ your eyes.

9. **fugitive** *(adj.)* running away or escaping; *(n.)* someone who is running away from the law

   We have finally captured the _____fugitive_____ chicken thief.

   The police are searching for a dangerous _____fugitive_____.

10. **hesitant** *(adj.)* 1. holding back; 2. not able to decide

    Why are you so _____hesitant_____ to jump in the pool?

11. indifferent *(adj.)* 1. having no interest in; 2. having no feeling about or opinion of

She was _____indifferent_____ to his pleas and cries for mercy, and she grounded him.

12. laborious *(adj.)* requiring or involving hard work or effort

The group worked for two weeks with _____laborious_____ intensity.

13. monopoly *(n.)* complete control of a business or service by one group

That company used to have a _____monopoly_____ , but now there are several different telephone companies.

14. optical *(adj.)* of or having to do with eyes and eyesight

McKinley decided to have an _____optical_____ exam.

15. portray *(v.)* 1. to make a picture of; 2. to describe in words; 3. to act out onstage

The inspector tried to _____portray_____ the situation in a positive light.

16. recluse *(n.)* someone who lives apart from others; *(adj.)* apart from others; solitary

After the accident, Joe turned into a _____recluse_____ .

Sometimes I dream of a _____recluse_____ existence in the mountains.

17. sedate *(adj.)* calm; settled; composed

This is a fairly _____sedate_____ crowd compared to last year's.

18. static *(adj.)* 1. having no motion; 2. at rest; *(n.)* 1. atmospheric electricity; 2. interference with radio or TV reception due to electric disturbance; 3. strong opposition

You can't ask a baby to hold a _____static_____ pose for that long.

We couldn't hear the radio program because of all the _____static_____ .

19. transact *(v.)* to do, to carry out, or to perform business

The officers have met to _____transact_____ a business deal.

20. wane *(v.)* to gradually decrease in size or amount; *(n.)* a gradual decrease or lessening

The fox's interest in the squirrel began to _____wane_____ .

Tonight the moon is on the _____wane_____ .

Use Your Vocabulary

Choose the word from the Word List that best completes each sentence. Write the word on the line. You may use the plural form of nouns and the past tense of verbs if necessary.

Last summer, I chose to compete with Alex, the **1** kid on the block. I didn't try to beat him at basketball, but at business. I interfered with his **2** on the neighborhood lawn-mowing market.

The idea came to me one hot day. My buddy Tyler and I were sitting on the porch, **3** because we had no money. Just then, Alex walked by and stapled a flyer to a telephone pole. According to his flyer, his business is **4** of mowing lawns, trimming hedges, and weeding gardens. The sign **5** my melting brain.

"That's it!" I said. "We can mow lawns too." Tyler just shrugged and looked **6** .

"Come on, Ty," I persisted. "We could have a(n) **7** summer. Think of the cash we could make!"

"I don't know." He sounded **8** . "Mowing lawns in the hot sun sounds awfully **9** . Besides, who'll hire us? Alex does all the yards around here."

"Ty," I said. "A few lawns a week won't **10** you. And I know where to start. Alex doesn't work for Mr. Maloney." Tyler, normally very **11** , jumped away from me and looked nervous.

"There's no way I'm going near that house!"

Mr. Maloney lives in an old, peeling house on the corner. He's been a(n) **12** for 20 years. The kids all **13** him as a deformed and dangerous **14** hiding from the FBI. I could see Tyler's interest in earning money begin to **15** . He **16** himself from the entire project, so I went down to the corner by myself.

I knocked on his door and waited. The entire house remained **17** . Finally, the door opened. For a moment, I could only stare. Was this a(n) **18** illusion? I saw before me a smiling, grey-haired man.

"I'm sorry I took so long," Mr. Maloney said. "I was **19** on the phone. How can I help you?" I told him I'd come to **20** a business deal. He invited me in for lemonade, and he became the first of my many customers that summer.

1. _____ dominant

2. _____ monopoly

3. _____ despondent

4. _____ comprised

5. _____ agitated

6. _____ indifferent

7. _____ bounteous

8. _____ hesitant

9. _____ laborious

10. _____ fatigue

11. _____ sedate

12. _____ recluse

13. _____ portray

14. _____ fugitive

15. _____ wane

16. _____ disassociated

17. _____ static

18. _____ optical

19. _____ engaged

20. _____ transact

SYNONYMS

Synonyms are words that have the same or nearly the same meanings.

Part 1 Choose the word from the box that is the best synonym for each group of words. Write the word on the line.

comprise	despondent	dominant	fugitive
hesitant	indifferent	transact	wane

1. reluctant, unsure, faltering _____ hesitant

2. fleeing; runaway, outlaw _____ fugitive

3. diminish, fade; decline _____ wane

4. governing, prevailing, primary _____ dominant

5. depressed, melancholy, hopeless _____ despondent

6. consist of, include _____ comprise

7. nonchalant, unconcerned, detached _____ indifferent

8. conduct, negotiate, deal _____ transact

Part 2 Replace the underlined word with a word from the box that means the same or almost the same. Write your answer on the line.

agitate	engaged	fatigue	static
portray	optical	recluse	

9. In his story, Jude chose to <u>depict</u> the man as a wretched villain.
   _____ portray

10. My cousin is <u>betrothed</u> to a movie star. _____ engaged

11. Zach is having <u>visual</u> problems lately. _____ optical

12. Don't <u>disturb</u> the baby, or he'll never go back to sleep. _____ agitate

13. Our neighbor is turning into a <u>hermit</u>; we haven't seen her in weeks.
   _____ recluse

14. The circles under her eyes showed her <u>exhaustion</u>. _____fatigue_____

15. We are hoping to spend a <u>quiet</u> evening at home. _____static_____

 ## ANTONYMS

Antonyms are words that have opposite or nearly opposite meanings.

Part 1 Choose the word from the box that is the best antonym for each group of words. Write the word on the line.

> agitate   comprise   despondent   sedate   wane

1. exclude, lack   _____comprise_____

2. upset, ruffled, frantic   _____sedate_____

3. still, quiet, calm   _____agitate_____

4. lighthearted, happy, elated   _____despondent_____

5. enlarge, grow; increase   _____wane_____

Part 2 Replace the underlined word with a word from the box that means the opposite or almost the opposite. Write your answer on the line.

> laborious   engaged   fatigue   indifferent   hesitant

6. Anne is the most <u>involved</u> member of the team. _____indifferent_____

7. The clown's <u>liveliness</u> is contagious. _____fatigue_____

8. Are you <u>available</u> on Friday afternoon? _____engaged_____

9. We noticed his extremely <u>confident</u> manner right away. _____hesitant_____

10. It's really an <u>effortless</u> task. _____laborious_____

WORD STUDY

Root Words Write the word from the box that has most to do with each described profession.

> dialogue   eulogy   logistics
>
> monologue   technology   zoology

1. one who works to protect endangered animals _____zoology_____

2. a preacher, especially at a funeral _____euology_____

3. a writer of novels or short stories _____dialogue_____

4. a computer engineer _____technology_____

5. a person who plans all the details of a big wedding _____logistics_____

6. a comedian _____monologue_____

> ## Vocabulary in Action
>
> In order to stretch your word knowledge, look at each word in the Word Study box and identify its part of speech. Then try to figure out what you need to do to make the word function as a different part of speech. For example, the word **dialogue** is most often a noun, occasionally a verb. If you change the word to *dialogic*, you create an adjective.

CHALLENGE WORDS

Word Learning—Challenge!

Study the spelling, part of speech, and meaning(s) of each word. Complete each sentence by writing the word on the line. Then read the sentence.

1. **arbitrary** *(adj.)* 1. existing or occurring by chance; 2. based on one's own judgment, without restriction

   You can't just make _____**arbitrary**_____ changes to the rules.

2. **conspicuous** *(adj.)* attracting attention by being unusual

   Please don't make any _____**conspicuous**_____ noises during the concert.

3. **envisage** *(v.)* to imagine or visualize

   How do you _____**envisage**_____ your future?

4. **lackadaisical** *(adj.)* showing little or no interest or energy

   Peggy's _____**lackadaisical**_____ approach to her schoolwork frustrated her teachers.

5. **optimum** *(n.)* something that is most favorable; *(adj.)* best or most favorable

   Among film ratings, four stars is the _____**optimum**_____.

   This critic rarely gives a film the _____**optimum**_____ rating.

Use Your Vocabulary—Challenge!

Summer Job Description It's summertime! You have been wanting to earn extra money, and you've found your dream job for the summer. Write a story about your job, using the five Challenge Words above.

> ### *Vocabulary in Action*
>
> Because English is a living language, more words are being added to it all the time. Some slang expressions you know today might someday be the source of a legitimate word.
>
> This is the origin of the whimsical word ***lackadaisical***, which first appeared in English around 1768. It comes from the interjection *lackadaisy*, "alas, alack," and is an alteration of *lack-a-day* (1695). One who cried "lack-a-day" was considered sentimental.

FUN WITH WORDS

Write an advertisement for a summer business you'd like to start. Tell people what you can do for them and why they should hire you. Use at least 10 vocabulary words from this chapter in your ad.

Answers will vary.

WORD LIST

Read each word using the pronunciation key.

agonize (ag´ ə nīz)
bravado (brə vä´ dō)
confer (kən fər´)
detention (di ten´ shən)
discipline (dis´ ə plən)
drone (drōn)
engineer (en jə nēr´)
feat (fēt)
fundamental (fun də men´ təl)
hoard (hôrd)
infinite (in´ fə nit)
lament (lə ment´)
multitude (mul´ tə tōōd)
optimistic (op tə mis´ tik)
pragmatic (prag mat´ ik)
recourse (rē´ kôrs)
sequence (sē´ kwəns)
stimulate (stim´ yə lāt)
transit (tran´ zit)
weary (wēr´ ē)

WORD STUDY

Prefixes

The prefix *mis-* means "bad, badly," or "wrongly."

misanthrope (mis´ ən thrōp) *(n.)* one who does not trust people
misbehave (mis bi hāv´) *(v.)* to behave badly
misfortune (mis fôr´ chən) *(n.)* bad luck
misspell (mis spel´) *(v.)* to spell incorrectly
mistake (mis stāk´) *(v.)* to wrongly identify; *(n.)* an error
misunderstand (mis un dər stand´) *(v.)* to not understand or comprehend

Challenge Words

gesticulate (jes tik´ yōō lāt)
juxtapose (juks´ tə pōz)
ostentatious (os ten tā´ shəs)
premise (prem´ is)
resilient (ri zil´ yənt)

■ **TEACHER TIP:** See page ix for suggestions on how to use this page.

Read each sentence below to figure out the meaning of the word in **bold**. Use reasoning skills and the remainder of the sentence to help you. Write the meaning of the word on the line.

1. When the **weary** traveler finally made it home, she collapsed into bed.

   tired; having fatigue

2. I mailed your letter last week; it must still be in **transit**.

   passage over, across, or through

3. The committee will meet to **confer** about the proposed changes to the lunchroom policy.

   to discuss together; to share ideas

4. To teach your dog **discipline**, begin training while it's a puppy.

   behavior that follows rules

5. The band played in Central Park before a **multitude** of fans.

   a great, indefinite number

6. The tightrope walker enthralled the crowd with his skill and **bravado**.

   a showy display of courage or bravery

7. The **drone** visited several flowers and then flew back to the hive.

   a male bee

8. The appearance of Cass's story in the magazine was quite a **feat** for her.

   an act of hard work, strength, or great accomplishment

9. Lada kept a **hoard** of DVDs she wouldn't let us use.

   a hidden supply of something stored for future use

10. My only **recourse** was to take the broken MP3 player to the store manager.

    the ability to turn to someone or something for help

WORD MEANINGS

Word Learning

Study the spelling, part(s) of speech, and meaning(s) of each word. Complete each sentence by writing the word on the line. Then read the sentence.

1. **agonize** *(v.)* 1. to suffer great physical or emotional pain; 2. to make a major effort

   You don't have to _____ agonize _____ over this decision.

2. **bravado** *(n.)* a showy display of courage or bravery

   Underneath his _____ bravado _____, I think he's nervous.

3. **confer** *(v.)* 1. to discuss together; 2. to share ideas

   Why don't you _____ confer _____ with your teacher about your grade?

4. **detention** *(n.)* 1. the act of delaying or keeping behind; 2. the condition of being held behind

   Mr. Jeffreys chose to enforce the _____ detention _____ of students after class.

5. **discipline** *(n.)* 1. training to learn or improve; 2. behavior that follows rules of conduct; *(v.)* 1. to drill or train by instruction; 2. to punish

   I think Sari has the _____ discipline _____ required to become a great dancer.

   The captain really knows how to _____ discipline _____ her troops.

6. **drone** *(v.)* to make a constant dull humming sound; *(n.)* 1. a dull humming sound; 2. a male bee

   I can hear the engines _____ drone _____ from here.

   I couldn't sleep because of the _____ drone _____ of a car alarm outside.

7. **engineer** *(n.)* 1. a person who designs or builds an operating system; 2. one who operates an engine; *(v.)* to plan, build, or manage

   We will need an _____ engineer _____ to design and build the new bridge.

   Here is the fellow who will _____ engineer _____ the new playground.

8. **feat** *(n.)* an act of hard work, strength, or great accomplishment

   The acrobat prepared for several months for the performance of her crowning _____ feat _____ on the trapeze.

9. **fundamental** *(adj.)* of a foundation or basis; basic; *(n.)* an essential or important part

The vote of the people is _____fundamental_____ to a democracy.

The relationship between a subject and verb is a _____fundamental_____ of grammar.

10. **hoard** *(n.)* a hidden supply of something stored for future use; *(v.)* to gather by saving or hiding

I'll have to reach into my _____hoard_____ of chocolate bars.

Squirrels begin to _____hoard_____ nuts and seeds long before winter begins.

11. **infinite** *(adj.)* having no boundaries or limit; endless

My uncle seems to have an _____infinite_____ supply of stories to tell.

12. **lament** *(n.)* a song or poem of grief; *(v.)* 1. to feel or show grief; 2. to regret deeply

Mara sang a bitter _____lament_____ of a lost love.

We all _____lament_____ the loss of our good friend.

13. **multitude** *(n.)* a great, indefinite number

Vicky gazed up into the _____multitude_____ of stars.

14. **optimistic** *(adj.)* likely to expect the best result or outcome

I am not too _____optimistic_____ about finishing on time.

15. **pragmatic** *(adj.)* having a practical point of view

Jim is no dreamer; he always gives very _____pragmatic_____ suggestions.

16. **recourse** *(n.)* an instance of turning to someone or something for help

My only _____recourse_____ was to ask the librarian for help.

17. **sequence** *(n.)* 1. the following of one thing after another; 2. a particular order

We must perform the tasks in their correct _____sequence_____.

18. **stimulate** *(v.)* to move or rouse to action

TV does not _____stimulate_____ your mind the way a book does.

19. **transit** *(n.)* passage over, across, or through

The package was lost in _____transit_____ somewhere.

20. **weary** *(adj.)* tired; having fatigue

I am _____weary_____ of all this arguing.

Use Your Vocabulary

Choose the word from the Word List that best completes each sentence. Write the word on the line. You may use the plural form of nouns and the past tense of verbs if necessary.

I went sailing for the first time last week, which was no small __1__ for me. I've always been afraid of boats. When Teri and her brother asked me if I would join them, I smiled and said with __2__, "Oh, I love to sail," although I was secretly terrified. For a week I __3__ over my decision. How could I back out of the situation? I __4__ with my friend Sarah, who told me to go. Ever __5__, she told me I'd have a great time breathing in the sea air. I am more __6__, however, and I just wanted to avoid seasickness.

The day of the sail I woke up early and began to panic. What if something went wrong? A(n) __7__ of possible catastrophes ran through my head. What if it rained? What if the boat capsized? I filled my backpack with a towel and dry clothes. I also packed my __8__ of dimes and quarters—just in case I needed money. I kept thinking of the __9__ possibilities for disaster. How could I cancel? I could tell them later that I'd had to serve a Saturday __10__. But I knew that I had no __11__, and __12__ with worry, I left the house to meet Teri and her brother.

I rode my bike to the dock, using all my self-__13__. Teri showed me how to climb onto the boat, and before I knew it, we were under way. I began to __14__ the loss of solid ground under my feet. Teri noticed my white knuckles gripping the edge of the seat. "Don't worry," she said. "This boat is __15__ for safety, and my brother is a great sailor."

Gradually, I relaxed my grip as I watched the other two perform the __16__ of steps necessary to raise the sails. Soon we were in smooth __17__ across the lake. I listened to the peaceful, faraway __18__ of an airplane. I really began to enjoy myself!

When we docked the boat, I said to Teri, "Well, you've __19__ my interest. Do you think your brother could teach me the __20__ of sailing?"

1. _____ feat
2. _____ bravado
3. _____ agonized
4. _____ conferred
5. _____ optimistic
6. _____ pragmatic
7. _____ multitude
8. _____ hoard
9. _____ infinite
10. _____ detention
11. _____ recourse
12. _____ weary
13. _____ discipline
14. _____ lament
15. _____ engineered
16. _____ sequence
17. _____ transit
18. _____ drone
19. _____ stimulated
20. _____ fundamentals

 **SYNONYMS**

Synonyms are words that have the same or nearly the same meanings.

Part 1 Choose the word from the box that is the best synonym for each group of words. Write the word on the line.

detention	bravado	agonize	engineer
lament	stimulate	recourse	pragmatic

1. struggle, endure _____ agonize

2. mourn, sorrow _____ lament

3. heroics, swaggering, blustering _____ bravado

4. constraint, confinement _____ detention

5. planner, builder; design _____ engineer

6. rational, logical, reasonable _____ pragmatic

7. appeal, resource, refuge _____ recourse

8. excite, incite, agitate _____ stimulate

Part 2 Replace the underlined word(s) with a word from the box that means the same or almost the same. Write your answer on the line.

hoard	transit	feat	infinite
confer	sequence	weary	

9. My sisters and I will <u>consult</u> about what to buy for Mom's birthday.
    _____ confer

10. Jake can always dip into his <u>stash</u> of money. _____ hoard

11. He seems to have an <u>endless</u> supply of excuses. _____ infinite

12. We are all proud of your great academic <u>achievement</u>. _____ feat

13. Can we rehearse the scenes in the <u>right order</u>? _____ sequence

14. The <u>worn-out</u> horse fell asleep at the stable door. _____ weary

15. She is terribly busy visiting people; she's always in <u>motion</u>. _____ transit

Chapter 11   Level H

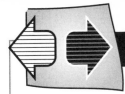

ANTONYMS

Antonyms are words that have opposite or nearly opposite meanings.

Part 1 Choose the word from the box that is the best antonym for each group of words. Write the word on the line.

> stimulate   bravado   agonize   drone   infinite

1. enjoy, celebrate, relax   _____agonize_____

2. finite, definite, measurable   _____infinite_____

3. deaden, paralyze, stun   _____stimulate_____

4. shriek; high-pitched sound   _____drone_____

5. cowardice, fear, modesty   _____bravado_____

Part 2 Replace the underlined word with a word from the box that means the opposite or almost the opposite. Write your answer on the line.

> multitude   lament   pragmatic   optimistic   lament

6. When we heard that our neighbors were leaving, we began to <u>rejoice</u>.
   _____lament_____

7. If you want gadgets, we have a <u>few</u>. _____multitude_____

8. George has a very <u>idealistic</u> approach to solving problems. _____pragmatic_____

9. It's a real challenge to work with such an <u>energetic</u> group. _____weary_____

10. No matter where we are, my father always has a <u>pessimistic</u> outlook.
    _____optimistic_____

Vocabulary in Action

Most cities in the United States were built around the automobile. In many places, public transportation, or mass *transit,* is not available. Even large cities often lack reliable public transportation. One exception is New York City, the only city in America where more than half the people do not own an automobile. About 33 percent of the nation's mass transportation riders live in or near New York City. Other major U.S. cities that boast solid public transit systems are Boston, Chicago, San Francisco, and Washington, D.C.

WORD STUDY

Prefixes Choose the word from the box that best completes each of the following sentences.

misanthrope	misbehave	misunderstand
misfortune	misspell	mistake

1. Raffaella hates it when people _____ misspell _____ her name.

2. Matt promised not to _____ misbehave _____ while his parents were away.

3. Don't be surprised if she makes nasty comments; she's a real _____ misanthrope _____.

4. Try not to _____ mistake _____ one twin for the other.

5. Speak clearly so I don't _____ misunderstand _____ what you are saying.

6. As I watched our empty boat float away, I could not believe our _____ misfortune _____.

Vocabulary in Action

Philosophy, literature, art, and music are full of **misanthropes**. In literature, one of the most famous misanthropes is Moliére's character Alceste, the protagonist of the 1666 play *The Misanthrope*.

In the play, Alceste rejects his culture's polite social conventions. This makes him extremely unpopular. Alceste sums up his attitude with the statement "Mankind has grown so base, I mean to break with the whole human race." However, his determination to reject society is countered by his desire to share a life with the lovely Célimène, whose actions oppose all he stands for.

CHALLENGE WORDS

Word Learning—Challenge!

Study the spelling, part of speech, and meaning(s) of each word. Complete each sentence by writing the word on the line. Then read the sentence.

1. **gesticulate** *(v.)* to create motions with the hands to show feeling or add force to what one is saying

   When the mayor speaks publicly, she _____gesticulates_____ and speaks with authority.

2. **juxtapose** *(v.)* to place close together or side by side

   For contrast, she chose to _____juxtapose_____ pictures of Texas and Alaska.

3. **ostentatious** *(adj.)* done for show; intended to attract attention

   I am tired of her _____ostentatious_____ displays of wealth.

4. **premise** *(n.)* an assumption that is taken for granted but not proved

   We are working on the _____premise_____ that the show won't start on time.

5. **resilient** *(adj.)* having the ability to recover or adjust to change

   Always _____resilient_____, he dried his tears and started over.

Use Your Vocabulary—Challenge!

A Sailor's Story Lucia Lemon is a champion sailor who has sailed around the world several times. She is the best sailor there is, and she knows it. Her archrival, Gwen Grape, has challenged her to a race. Use the five Challenge Words above to write a story about the race between Lucia and Gwen.

> ### Vocabulary in Action
>
> In logic, a **premise** (ca. 1374) is a "previous proposition from which another follows." It comes from the Middle Latin word *premissa*—"the proposition set before."

FUN WITH WORDS

Each of the following names has a vocabulary word from this chapter hidden in it. Underline the chapter words in the names.

1. Mag O'<u>Nizer</u>

2. B. R. <u>Avadon</u>

3. Fred <u>Rone</u>

4. Ben G. <u>Ineer</u>son

5. Mare <u>Coursen</u>

6. K. <u>W. Eary</u>

7. Louise <u>Quencen</u>

8. Chad I. <u>Sciplinee</u>

9. Misti <u>Mulatec</u>

10. Lin F. <u>Initer</u>

Now make up your own names with the following vocabulary words hidden in them.

Answers will vary.

11. detention _____

12. transit _____

13. pragmatic _____

14. feat _____

15. lament _____

16. confer _____

17. fundamental _____

18. hoard _____

19. multitude _____

20. optimistic _____

> ### Notable Quotes
>
> "Some of the world's greatest **feats** were accomplished by people not smart enough to know they were impossible."
>
> —Doug Larson (1902–1981), British middle-distance runner

© Loyola Press.

CHAPTER 12

WORD LIST

Read each word using the pronunciation key.

allocate (al´ ə kāt)
brim (brim)
conform (kən fôrm´)
dethrone (dē thrōn´)
disconnected (dis kə nek´ tid)
dubious (doo´ bē əs)
entitle (in tīt´ əl)
ferocious (fə rō´ shəs)
furlough (fər´ lō)
horizontal (hôr ə zän´ təl)
inkling (iŋk´ liŋ)
laud (lôd)
murmur (mər´ mər)
ordeal (ôr dēl´)
precise (pri sīs´)
rectify (rek´ tə fī)
shirk (shərk)
stoic (stō´ ik)
tumult (too´ mult)
wrath (rath)

WORD STUDY

Suffixes

The suffix *-ment* means "the act or state of" or "means of."

amazement (a māz´ mənt) *(n.)* the state of being amazed
commitment (kə mit´ mənt) *(n.)* the act of committing or pledging to do something in the future
employment (em ploi´ mənt) *(n.)* the state of being employed
monument (mon´ yə mənt) *(n.)* a memorial erected as a means of remembering a person or an event
ornament (ôr´ nə mənt) *(n.)* an object or a feature used as decoration
payment (pā´ mənt) *(n.)* the act of paying

Challenge Words

affirmation (af ər mā´ shən)
auspicious (ô spi´ shəs)
demeanor (di mēn´ ər)
enormity (e nôr´ mə tē)
prerogative (pri räg´ ə tiv)

© Loyola Press.

129

Level H

■ **TEACHER TIP:** See page ix for suggestions on how to use this page.

Read each sentence below to figure out the meaning of the word in **bold**. Use reasoning skills and the remainder of the sentence to help you. Write the meaning of the word on the line.

1. We stood on the **brim** of the canyon and looked down into the valley.

   the upper edge of anything hollow

2. The judges will surely **laud** your brilliant attempts to create electricity from water.

   to praise or glorify

3. The newspaper will **rectify** the error by reprinting the article without the mistakes.

   to make right

4. Fearing the **wrath** of the storm, we huddled in the basement.

   violent anger or rage

5. The club has decided to **allocate** the money to buy decorations for the fall carnival.

   to set aside for a special purpose

6. If the bottom half of the box doesn't **conform** to the top half, it won't close.

   to be or make similar in form

7. This ticket will **entitle** you to one ride on the roller coaster.

   to give a claim or right to; to qualify

8. From backstage, the actors could hear the **murmur** of the audience.

   a low, unclear, constant sound

9. Mrs. Merten took **precise** measurements so our uniforms would fit perfectly.

   exact

10. My brother is home from the army on a two-week **furlough**.

    time away; a leave of absence or vacation

WORD MEANINGS

Word Learning

Study the spelling, part(s) of speech, and meaning(s) of each word. Complete each sentence by writing the word on the line. Then read the sentence.

1. **allocate** *(v.)* to set aside for a special purpose

   The school chose to _____allocate_____ money for a new gym.

2. **brim** *(n.)* the upper edge of anything hollow

   Don't fill my cup to the _____brim_____.

3. **conform** *(v.)* 1. to be or make similar in form; 2. to act in harmony with; to comply

   My brother doesn't like to _____conform_____ to anyone else's ideas.

4. **dethrone** *(v.)* to remove from a position of power

   There was a movement to _____dethrone_____ the king.

5. **disconnected** *(adj.)* 1. apart from; 2. not connected

   I _____disconnected_____ my telephone so I could get some sleep.

6. **dubious** *(adj.)* doubtful or full of uncertainty

   She gave me a _____dubious_____ look and said, "Are you sure about that?"

7. **entitle** *(v.)* 1. to give a particular name or title to; 2. to give a claim or right to; 3. to qualify

   Do you think your ideas _____entitle_____ you to special treatment?

8. **ferocious** *(adj.)* 1. fierce or savage; 2. extreme or severe

   In the cave, there lived a _____ferocious_____ beast.

9. **furlough** *(n.)* 1. time away; 2. a leave of absence or vacation

   Her supervisors granted her a two-week _____furlough_____.

10. **horizontal** *(adj.)* parallel to the ground; *(n.)* something that goes across

    The carpenters laid a _____horizontal_____ beam across the hole in the floor.

    Mr. Martinek drew a _____horizontal_____ line across the top of the graph.

11. **inkling** *(n.)* 1. a hint; a slight suggestion; 2. a vague understanding

    I don't have the slightest _____inkling_____ of what you're talking about.

12. **laud** *(v.)* to praise or glorify

    Hundreds of people came to _____laud_____ the new king.

13. murmur *(n.)* a low, unclear, constant sound; *(v.)* to make a low, unclear, constant sound

From my bedroom, I could hear the _____murmur_____ of the stream.

In her sleep, my sister began to _____murmur_____ something about lunch.

14. ordeal *(n.)* a difficult or painful experience

I don't know how she will survive this _____ordeal_____.

15. precise *(adj.)* 1. clearly and carefully stated; 2. distinct; 3. exact

We gave _____precise_____ directions to the park from the school.

16. rectify *(v.)* to make right

How will you _____rectify_____ the situation?

17. shirk *(v.)* to put off work or duty in order to avoid

I hope you don't _____shirk_____ your responsibilities while I'm gone.

18. stoic *(adj.)* not showing feeling; restrained or impassive

She wore a _____stoic_____ expression on her face through the entire funeral.

19. tumult *(n.)* 1. a loud disturbance of a large crowd; 2. any confusion of the mind or feelings

The fight on the soccer field caused a _____tumult_____ among the crowd.

20. wrath *(n.)* violent anger or rage

Woe to the poor mortal on whom Zeus unleashes his _____wrath_____!

Vocabulary in Action

How did Pennsylvania get its name? Its founder, English reformer William Penn, named it in honor of his father.

Persecuted in England for refusing to renounce his Quaker faith and *conform* to the rules of the Anglican church, Penn came to America in 1682 and established Pennsylvania as a place where people could practice religion freely. The colony became a haven for minority religious sects from Germany, Holland, Scandinavia, and Great Britain.

In a 1682 document, Penn guaranteed absolute freedom of worship in Pennsylvania. Rich in fertile lands as well as religious freedom, the colony attracted settlers and grew rapidly. Thanks to William Penn, Pennsylvania, which guaranteed religious freedom for its citizens, was established in the New World.

Use Your Vocabulary

Choose the word from the Word List that best completes each sentence. Write the word on the line. You may use the plural form of nouns and the past tense of verbs if necessary.

In social studies class, we **1** the achievements of women in history. Our teacher felt that we were too **2** from the past and wanted to give us at least a(n) **3** of the women who have contributed to our world. Each student reached over the **4** of a bowl and pulled out the name of a famous woman. Then we had to write a short report. We responded at first with **5** of discontent, but once we got started, we were really interested by the women and some of the **6** they survived.

Many of these women chose not to **7** to the typical expectations. Deborah Sampson Gannett dressed as a man and fought with **8** bravery in the Revolutionary War. Another warrior, Ladshmi Bai, led Indian troops to fight those who wanted to **9** the king of the small kingdom of Jhansi.

Although no blood may be shed, political battles can become **10** as well. Elizabeth Cady Stanton caused a(n) **11** in the late 1800s by declaring to a(n) **12** public that women should be **13** to vote. She and her friend Susan B. Anthony **14** much of their time in the attempt to **15** this injustice. They inspired the **16** of many men and conservative women, but in 1920, the 19th Amendment to the Constitution let women vote.

Women have made contributions to science and the arts as well. Polish physicist Marie Curie's **17** scientific research led to the discovery of two elements—polonium and radium. Painter Georgia O'Keeffe used her paintings to capture the **18** lines and distinct colors of the New Mexico landscape.

Many women have worked in politics. Congresswoman Shirley Chisholm took an extended **19** from her political career to become a professor, encouraging women to go into politics. When Corazón Aquino's husband was killed, she did not **20** her duty. She became the next president of the Philippines.

1. _____ lauded
2. _____ disconnected
3. _____ inkling
4. _____ brim
5. _____ murmurs
6. _____ ordeals
7. _____ conform
8. _____ stoic
9. _____ dethrone
10. _____ ferocious
11. _____ tumult
12. _____ dubious
13. _____ entitled
14. _____ allocated
15. _____ rectify
16. _____ wrath
17. _____ precise
18. _____ horizontal
19. _____ furlough
20. _____ shirk

SYNONYMS

Synonyms are words that have the same or nearly the same meanings.

Part 1 Choose the word from the box that is the best synonym for each group of words. Write the word on the line.

conform	laud	entitle	disconnected
ordeal	precise	rectify	wrath

1. frenzy, rage, fury   _____wrath_____

2. difficulty, strain, trial   _____ordeal_____

3. definite, well-defined, accurate   _____precise_____

4. correct, improve, repair   _____rectify_____

5. agree, match, modify   _____conform_____

6. detached, separated, distant   _____disconnected_____

7. label, allow, permit   _____entitle_____

8. compliment, applaud, extol   _____laud_____

Part 2 Replace the underlined word with a word from the box that means the same or almost the same. Write your answer on the line.

allocate	brim	dubious	ferocious
inkling	shirk	tumult	

9. I came home with a <u>wild</u> hunger. _____ferocious_____

10. I have a <u>suspicion</u> that she's never been here before. _____inkling_____

11. Due to the <u>suspicious</u> nature of the man's complaints, the judge dismissed the case. _____dubious_____

12. Mark's confession has caused quite a <u>stir</u>. _____tumult_____

13. I chipped my tooth on the <u>rim</u> of the mug. _____brim_____

14. Every year we <u>earmark</u> part of our budget for entertainment.

_____allocate_____

15. At the beginning of summer vacation, he began to <u>neglect</u> his chores at home.

_____shirk_____

 **ANTONYMS**

Antonyms are words that have opposite or nearly opposite meanings.

Part 1 Choose the word from the box that is the best antonym for each group of words. Write the word on the line.

conform	entitle	dubious	stoic	disconnected

1. deprive, disallow _____entitle_____

2. certain, sure, positive _____dubious_____

3. emotional, feeling, indulgent _____stoic_____

4. together, united, joined, connected _____disconnected_____

5. conflict, differ, disagree _____conform_____

Part 2 Replace the underlined word with a word from the box that means the opposite or almost the opposite. Write your answer on the line.

ferocious	horizontal	laud	murmur	precise

6. The people will <u>condemn</u> her methods of ruling. _____laud_____

7. I stifled a <u>mild</u> desire to shout out loud. _____ferocious_____

8. I heard the mother <u>shout</u> something to her child. _____murmur_____

9. Everyone noticed his <u>careless</u> movements on the dance floor.

_____precise_____

10. Adam set down the ironing board in a <u>vertical</u> position. _____horizontal_____

WORD STUDY

Suffixes Decide which of the words from the box could be used in each sentence to replace the underlined word. Write the word on the line.

amazement	commitment	employment
monument	ornament	payment

1. I couldn't find any <u>work</u> the whole summer. ___employment___

2. Joe made a <u>promise</u> to finish the project. ___commitment___

3. To my <u>surprise</u>, everyone had gone home. ___amazement___

4. She has put her <u>check</u> in the mail already. ___payment___

5. We have removed every <u>decoration</u> from the tree. ___ornament___

6. The <u>statue</u> is visible from miles away. ___monument___

Vocabulary in Action

The Washington **Monument** in Washington, D.C., was completed on December 6, 1884. It is the focal point of the National Mall, as well as the background for concerts and fireworks.

How long did it take to complete the 555-foot Egyptian obelisk, topped with a 3,300-pound marble capstone and a 9-inch pyramid of cast aluminum? That question is harder to answer than it may seem. The Washington National Monument Society laid the monument's cornerstone in 1848 on Independence Day, 36 years before completion. But when the obelisk was at a height of about 156 feet, the society lost support and funding. The monument stood incomplete and untouched for 20 years.

Finally, in 1876, President Ulysses S. Grant authorized the U.S. Army Corps of Engineers to finish the project. When fully constructed, it was the world's tallest structure. Today, the approximately 36,000-stacked blocks of granite and marble compose the world's tallest freestanding masonry structure. The 9-inch aluminum pyramid, which completes the top of the structure as it narrows to a point, is 100 ounces of solid aluminum. Aluminum was a rare metal in the 1880s, selling for $1.10 per ounce. The pyramid was the largest piece of aluminum of its day.

CHALLENGE WORDS

Word Learning—Challenge!

Study the spelling, part(s) of speech, and meaning(s) of each word. Complete each sentence by writing the word on the line. Then read the sentence.

1. **affirmation** *(n.)* confirmation that something is correct

   She looked to her teacher for an _____affirmation_____ of her talents.

2. **auspicious** *(adj.)* showing promise of success or good fortune

   The club introduced its _____auspicious_____ leaders.

3. **demeanor** *(n.)* 1. outward manner; 2. behavior or conduct

   Libby's shy _____demeanor_____ made it hard to get to know her.

4. **enormity** *(n.)* extreme wickedness or atrocious character

   I don't think you understand the _____enormity_____ of the situation.

5. **prerogative** *(n.)* an exclusive or special right that belongs to a person or group

   If she wants to move to Mexico, that's her _____prerogative_____.

Use Your Vocabulary—Challenge!

Newspaper Article You are a journalist who is attending a city council meeting on the subject of the city parks. There is a group who believes that children should not be allowed to use public athletic fields without a permit. Use the five Challenge Words above to write an article about the meeting.

> ### Vocabulary in Action
>
> The word **auspicious** (ca. 1596) means "of good omen." It comes from the Latin *auspicium*, meaning "divination by observing the flight of birds."

FUN WITH WORDS

Use the clues to complete the puzzle. Choose from the vocabulary words in this chapter.

Across

2. going across
5. a confusion or stir
6. great anger
10. to make match
11. uncertain
13. to put aside for a certain thing
14. to avoid something

Down

1. a low, constant sound
3. to pay a compliment
4. showing no emotion
7. to permit
8. exact
9. time off
11. to remove a leader from power
12. a hard time

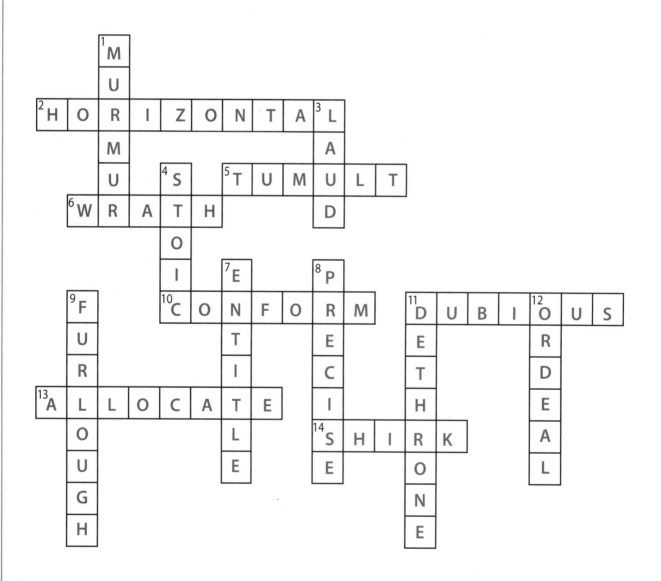

Review 10–12

Word Meanings Fill in the bubble of the word that is best defined by each phrase.

1. to move forcefully
   - a. hoard
   - **b. agitate**
   - c. lament
   - d. entitle

2. to make weary or exhaust
   - a. lament
   - b. wane
   - **c. fatigue**
   - d. murmur

3. a remarkable achievement
   - **a. feat**
   - b. tumult
   - c. furlough
   - d. detention

4. without beginning or end
   - a. precise
   - b. dubious
   - c. horizontal
   - **d. infinite**

5. a slight hint or suggestion
   - **a. inkling**
   - b. recluse
   - c. drone
   - d. brim

6. to leave undone what should be done
   - **a. shirk**
   - b. transact
   - c. rectify
   - d. discipline

7. to get smaller, weaker, or dimmer
   - a. stimulate
   - b. entitle
   - **c. wane**
   - d. allocate

8. looking at things in a matter-of-fact way
   - a. bounteous
   - **b. pragmatic**
   - c. sedate
   - d. fundamental

9. to be the same or similar
   - a. comprise
   - **b. conform**
   - c. confer
   - d. disassociate

10. to collect secretly and store away
    - a. dethrone
    - b. laud
    - c. agonize
    - **d. hoard**

11. to play the part of in a play or movie
    - **a. portray**
    - b. sedate
    - c. stimulate
    - d. laud

12. an unpleasant experience
    - a. fugitive
    - **b. ordeal**
    - c. feat
    - d. recourse

13. forced delay or confinement
    - a. recluse
    - b. fatigue
    - **c. detention**
    - d. wrath

14. wild and fierce
    - **a. ferocious**
    - b. optical
    - c. indifferent
    - d. dominant

15. giving more than enough
    - **a. bounteous**
    - b. pragmatic
    - c. weary
    - d. precise

16. to discuss thoughts and ideas
    - a. disassociate
    - **b. confer**
    - c. portray
    - d. transact

17. to mourn or grieve
a. lament **b.** shirk **c.** discipline **d.** rectify

18. not moving or changing
a. despondent **b.** stoic **c.** hesitant **d.** static

19. a steady flow of quiet, unclear sound
a. monopoly **b.** murmur **c.** wrath **d.** fugitive

20. passage through, across, or over
a. drone **b.** multitude **c.** transit **d.** brim

Sentence Completion Choose the word from the box that best completes each of the following sentences. Write the word in the blank.

> optical   rectify   furlough   indifferent   despondent
> disconnected   allocates   bravado   engineered   hesitant

1. I was __hesitant__ to accept my brother's seemingly innocent offer.

2. The designers __engineered__ the new system to work automatically.

3. Alex spent the day trying to __rectify__ a computer error.

4. Maggie took a(n) __furlough__ from her job and went to Australia for a month.

5. I bought my red-and-white striped glasses at the new __optical__ shop.

6. Stewart was __despondent__ when we didn't get the part in the play.

7. Pedro put on a good show of __bravado__ in front of the bully, but we knew he was really terrified.

8. The U.S. Congress __allocates__ funds to run the national parks.

9. Although I am physically __disconnected__ from my family, we talk daily.

10. Kayla's __indifferent__ attitude toward her grades shows in her sloppy work.

Fill in the Blanks Fill in the bubble of the pair of words that best completes each sentence.

1. As the boring TV show ____ on, my ____ got the best of me, and I fell asleep.
a. agonized, bravado **c.** engineered, furlough
b. allocated, static **d.** droned, fatigue

2. A(n) _____ is a person who does everything possible to _____ from other people.
- **a.** monopoly, dethrone
- **b.** ordeal, allocate
- **c.** recluse, disassociate
- **d.** transit, hoard

3. The group of _____ met to _____ about an exciting new design concept.
- **a.** engineers, confer
- **b.** inklings, conform
- **c.** recluses, murmur
- **d.** fugitives, agitate

4. Students who _____ their obligations in Mr. Sewell's class will find themselves in _____ in a hurry.
- **a.** shirk, detention
- **b.** portray, discipline
- **c.** allocate, furlough
- **d.** agonize, tumult

5. It's good to be _____ about the future, but you must be _____ too.
- **a.** ferocious, hesitant
- **b.** despondent, disconnected
- **c.** fundamental, precise
- **d.** optimistic, pragmatic

6. Andy hoped a show of _____ would make people think he was the _____ player on the team.
- **a.** discipline, dubious
- **b.** bravado, dominant
- **c.** fatigue, indifferent
- **d.** tumult, fundamental

7. How can anyone who is about to receive a two-week _____ be _____?
- **a.** ordeal, dubious
- **b.** engineer, indifferent
- **c.** furlough, despondent
- **d.** monopoly, hesitant

8. The winning ticket _____ you to receive a _____ of prizes.
- **a.** comprises, hoard
- **b.** entitles, multitude
- **c.** conforms, wrath
- **d.** agitates, feat

9. Mom had no _____ but to _____ us for staying out so late.
- **a.** bravado, comprise
- **b.** inkling, entitle
- **c.** sequence, fatigue
- **d.** recourse, discipline

10. The _____ wolf kept its place as leader by acting _____ around the other wolves in the pack.
- **a.** dominant, ferocious
- **b.** indifferent, agitated
- **c.** hesitant, fatigued
- **d.** optimistic, despondent

Classifying Words
Sort the words in the box by writing each word to complete a phrase in the correct category.

agitate	allocate	bounteous	bravado	conform
despondent	discipline	dominant	drone	entitled
ferocious	fugitive	hoard	infinite	laborious
multitude	murmur	precise	rectify	weary

Words You Might Use to Talk About Animal Behavior

1. dangerous to _____ agitate _____ the python's cage
2. _____ dominant _____ animal expecting to eat first
3. tiny dogs displaying lots of _____ bravado _____
4. _____ fugitive _____ coyote hiding in the woods
5. the bared teeth of a(n) _____ ferocious _____ lion

Words You Might Use to Talk About Engineers

6. each client _____ entitled _____ to personal attention
7. able to take _____ precise _____ measurements
8. the _____ discipline _____ to spend long hours studying
9. _____ conform _____ to the client's needs and expectations
10. be able to _____ rectify _____ flaws in the design

Words You Might Use to Talk About Sounds

11. the annoying _____ drone _____ of a buzzing fly in the window
12. _____ despondent _____ sobs over the broken heirloom
13. the _____ murmur _____ of secretive voices behind a closed door
14. ragged, _____ laborious _____ breathing of the winded runner
15. _____ weary _____ sigh from the baby's tired sitter

Words You Might Use to Talk About Amounts

16. cheered by the _____ bounteous _____ supply of good things to eat
17. hiding a(n) _____ hoard _____ of cookies in the back of a drawer
18. a(n) _____ infinite _____ number of stars on a clear night
19. a field that contains a(n) _____ multitude _____ of flowers
20. to _____ allocate _____ the shares of the profits fairly

WORD LIST

Read each word using the pronunciation key.

amiable (āˊ mē ə bəl)
brisk (brisk)
controversy (konˊ trə vər sē)
detract (di traktˊ)
discord (disˊ kôrd)
durable (do͝orˊ ə bəl)
envelop (en velˊ əp)
fervent (fərˊ vənt)
fury (fyo͝orˊ ē)
hostility (ho stilˊ i tē)
inquisitive (in kwizˊ ə tiv)
legible (lejˊ ə bəl)
mutilate (myo͞otˊ əl āt)
oscillate (osˊ ə lāt)
predator (predˊ ə tər)
reiterate (rē itˊ ə rāt)
siege (sēj)
subordination (sə bôr də nāˊ shən)
twinge (twinj)
wretched (rechˊ id)

WORD STUDY

Root Words

The root *man* or *manu* means "hand."

manacle (manˊ ə kel) *(n.)* handcuff
manage (manˊ ij) *(v.)* to take charge of; to supervise
manicure (manˊ i kyo͝or) *(n.)* a treatment for the care of the hands and fingernails
manipulate (mə nipˊ yə lāt) *(v.)* 1. to handle with skill; 2. to skillfully influence, often unfairly
manual (manˊ yo͞o əl) *(adj.)* 1. operated by hand; 2. of or requiring physical human effort
manuscript (manˊ yə skript) *(n.)* a text written by hand or computer

Challenge Words

gregarious (grə gârˊ ē əs)
mortify (môrˊ ti fī)
permeate (pərˊ mē āt)
ruminate (ro͞oˊ mə nāt)
sardonic (sär dänˊ ik)

■ **TEACHER TIP:** See page ix for suggestions on how to use this page.

Read each sentence below to figure out the meaning of the word in **bold**. Use reasoning skills and the remainder of the sentence to help you. Write the meaning of the word on the line.

1. As they grew older, the jealousy and **discord** between the two sisters gave way to a strong friendship.

   _____ lack of agreement _____

2. The lion is the most powerful **predator** on the plains of Africa.

   _____ an animal that attacks other animals or living things _____

3. I want a fan that **oscillates** so we can cool both sides of the room.

   _____ to swing back and forth _____

4. If you **mutilate** a library book by ripping its pages, the library will revoke your card.

   _____ to cut off, tear, or damage an important part of _____

5. Our server is busy and overworked; she doesn't deserve this kind of **hostility** from her customers.

   _____ unfriendliness; the state of being enemies _____

6. Did you hear me the first time, or should I **reiterate** my request?

   _____ to say over again; to repeat _____

7. Pam felt a **twinge** of regret as she saw her brother drive away.

   _____ a sudden emotional pain _____

8. I like to take a **brisk** walk after eating a big meal.

   _____ lively; quick; active _____

9. Her handwriting on the card was barely **legible**, so I asked her to read it to me.

   _____ able to be read _____

10. In Charles Dickens's novel *Oliver Twist*, the orphans lived in a **wretched** house and ate only gruel and water.

    _____ in very poor condition _____

WORD MEANINGS

Word Learning

Study the spelling, part of speech, and meaning(s) of each word. Complete each sentence by writing the word on the line. Then read the sentence.

1. **amiable** *(adj.)* 1. agreeable and friendly; 2. good-natured

   The United States has an _____amiable_____ relationship with many countries.

2. **brisk** *(adj.)* lively; quick; active

   She conducted the class at a _____brisk_____ pace.

3. **controversy** *(n.)* a disagreement or debate between opposing sides

   The newest postage stamps are a subject of great _____controversy_____.

4. **detract** *(v.)* 1. to lessen; 2. to take away a good part of something

   I hope my absence didn't _____detract_____ from all the fun.

5. **discord** *(n.)* 1. a lack of agreement; 2. a harsh noise

   The meeting consisted only of argument and _____discord_____; we accomplished nothing.

6. **durable** *(adj.)* 1. lasting; 2. able to withstand wear or weathering

   I need a good, _____durable_____ pair of boots for the winter.

7. **envelop** *(v.)* 1. to enclose with a wrap or cover; 2. to surround completely

   We waited for the coming fog to _____envelop_____ the house.

8. **fervent** *(adj.)* 1. showing great emotion or warmth; 2. ardent; 3. enthusiastic

   His most _____fervent_____ wish was to meet his favorite basketball player in person.

9. **fury** *(n.)* fierce anger or rage

   After I crashed her car, I could not bear to face her _____fury_____.

10. **hostility** *(n.)* 1. unfriendliness; the state of being enemies; 2. opposition to an idea

    The board of directors showed _____hostility_____ toward our new idea.

11. **inquisitive** *(adj.)* 1. extremely curious; 2. eager to learn

    Wyatt, our pet ferret, is an _____inquisitive_____ little fellow and gets into everything.

12. **legible** *(adj.)* 1. easily read; 2. apparent

When you hand in your next paper, please make it more _____legible_____.

13. **mutilate** *(v.)* to cut off, tear, or damage an important part of something

My baby sister manages to _____mutilate_____ any delicate thing that she touches.

14. **oscillate** *(v.)* to swing back and forth

I watched with fascination as the dolls in the shop window began to _____oscillate_____.

15. **predator** *(n.)* 1. an animal that attacks other animals or living things; 2. a person who attacks others

Because the deer have no natural _____predator_____ anymore, the population is growing.

16. **reiterate** *(v.)* to say over again; to repeat

Before we finish, I would like to _____reiterate_____ my point about the heavy traffic.

17. **siege** *(n.)* the surrounding of a location for the purpose of capture

The troops have brought the entire city under _____siege_____.

18. **subordination** *(n.)* 1. placement in a lower class or rank; 2. obedience

The king insisted upon the complete _____subordination_____ of the palace staff.

19. **twinge** *(n.)* 1. a sudden, sharp pain; 2. a sudden emotional pain

Every time I move my knee, I feel a _____twinge_____ of pain.

20. **wretched** *(adj.)* 1. living a miserable life; 2. in very poor condition

The old, _____wretched_____ house sat alone in the middle of the field.

Use Your Vocabulary

Choose the word from the Word List that best completes each sentence. Write the word on the line. You may use the plural form of nouns and the past tense of verbs if necessary.

I didn't mean to start a(n) __1__ , but no one thought I would beat the Kid at his best video game. The Kid, as he is commonly known, is a perfectly nice, __2__ person until it comes to video games. Then he becomes a vicious __3__ looking for innocent victims to devour. Before I begin, I'd like to __4__ that I didn't mean to start anything last Tuesday; it just happened.

It all started with a barely __5__ note in my locker. "Be at Tom's after school, or I'll come find you." Tom is our classmate, who regularly invites gamers to play at his home. The note was signed, "the Kid." I knew better than to ignore his tone of __6__ . If the Kid had picked me as his next opponent, then I had to show up. And besides, my __7__ nature led me to wonder why he had chosen me and how the event would play out. Might I even win? It was my __8__ hope that I would not.

Without meaning to __9__ from the Kid's reputation as a great player, I'll tell you now that I knew I was better. But I also knew that if I beat the Kid, he would unleash his __10__ on me. I did not cherish the idea of a(n) __11__ kick in the seat of the pants! Truly, I wanted to avoid all __12__ .

I arrived at Tom's place __13__ by a group of my buddies. They were to serve as protection in case the Kid decided to try and __14__ me. He waited for me in the living room.

"You __15__ creature," the Kid said as he eerily __16__ in a chair. "I hope you're made of __17__ stuff, because I'm gonna' pound you." We walked over to the console, and the game began.

It didn't last long. Within five minutes, I had his troops under __18__ . I felt only a(n) __19__ of regret as my generals and I demanded his __20__ . The Kid looked stunned. He hung his head for a minute and then looked up at me.

"Hey," he said. "What do you say you and me form a team? Together, we could beat everyone in town!"

1. _____ controversy
2. _____ amiable
3. _____ predator
4. _____ reiterate
5. _____ legible
6. _____ hostility
7. _____ inquisitive
8. _____ fervent
9. _____ detract
10. _____ fury
11. _____ brisk
12. _____ discord
13. _____ enveloped
14. _____ mutilate
15. _____ wretched
16. _____ oscillated
17. _____ durable
18. _____ siege
19. _____ twinge
20. _____ subordination

© Loyola Press.

SYNONYMS

Synonyms are words that have the same or nearly the same meanings.

Part 1 Choose the word from the box that is the best synonym for each group of words. Write the word on the line.

amiable	detract	fury	legible
controversy	discord	mutilate	twinge

1. cramp, spasm, pang _____ twinge _____

2. dispute, argument, quarrel _____ controversy _____

3. deform, mangle, cripple _____ mutilate _____

4. pleasant, social, benevolent _____ amiable _____

5. ferocity, wrath, ire _____ fury _____

6. conflict, clash, disharmony _____ discord _____

7. diminish, reduce, subtract _____ detract _____

8. plain, clear, understandable _____ legible _____

Part 2 Replace the underlined word with a word from the box that means the same or almost the same. Write your answer on the line.

brisk	durable	envelop	fervent
hostility	reiterate	wretched	

9. Her coat used to be so big that it would <u>enwrap</u> her. _____ envelop _____

10. Why do you treat me with such <u>antagonism</u>? _____ hostility _____

11. We stopped at the fence for a <u>quick</u> chat. _____ brisk _____

12. You may ask the teacher to <u>repeat</u> her instructions. _____ reiterate _____

13. The president issued an <u>impassioned</u> plea for help. _____ fervent _____

14. The photographs showed masses of <u>forlorn</u> people standing in line.
    _____ wretched _____

15. The paint that we put on the house should be <u>lasting</u>. _____ durable _____

Chapter 13   Level H

 **ANTONYMS**

Antonyms are words that have opposite or nearly opposite meanings.

Part 1 Choose the word from the box that is the best antonym for each group of words. Write the word on the line.

| detract | discord | durable | envelop | legible |

1. unwrap, expose, unveil   envelop

2. increase, add to, enhance   detract

3. unreadable, unclear, indistinct   legible

4. fragile, flimsy, weak   durable

5. agreement, accord, harmony   discord

Part 2 Replace the underlined word with a word from the box that means the opposite or almost the opposite. Write your answer on the line.

| amiable | brisk | fervent | inquisitive | wretched |

6. A prosperous young woman lives in that house. _____ wretched

7. The new student is most unconcerned about how our school works.
   _____ inquisitive

8. The two countries engaged in a series of hostile negotiations.
   _____ amiable

9. We did not expect such a cool response to our invitation. _____ fervent

10. Lisa and Sally went for a lazy walk along the river's edge. _____ brisk

> *Vocabulary in Action*
>
> The word **amiable** first appeared in English around 1350 and comes from those who spoke Old French. They adapted it from the Latin word *amicabilis*, meaning "friendly." *Amiable* has the same root as the feminine name *Amy*, which means "beloved."

WORD STUDY

Root Words Each of the words in the box originally comes from a related word in Latin. Sometimes it comes from a related word in another language that also has roots in Latin. Read the word histories below. Choose the word from the box that matches each history.

manacle	manicure	manual
manage	manipulate	manuscript

1. Latin *manuale* (something that can be held in the hand)   <u>manual</u>

2. Latin *manus* (hand) + Latin *cura* (care)   <u>manicure</u>

3. French *manicle* (handcuff)   <u>manacle</u>

4. Italian *maneggiare* (to handle or train, especially horses)   <u>manage</u>

5. Latin *manus* (hand) + Latin *scriptus* (written)   <u>manuscript</u>

6. French *manipuler* (to handle an apparatus)   <u>manipulate</u>

Vocabulary in Action

Harry Houdini was a master of illusion. He earned an international reputation as an escape artist who dramatically freed himself from ropes, shackles, and handcuffs, also known as **manacles**. He was married to Wilhelmina Rahner, who, as Beatrice Houdini, was his stage assistant. He performed on vaudeville and appeared in many motion pictures.

Houdini, originally named Erik Weisz, was born in 1874 in Budapest, Hungary. However, he claimed to have been born in Appleton, Wisconsin. Houdini died in Detroit, Michigan, on October 31, 1926.

CHALLENGE WORDS

Word Learning—Challenge!

Study the spelling, part of speech, and meaning(s) of each word. Complete each sentence by writing the word on the line. Then read the sentence.

1. **gregarious** *(adj.)* enjoying the company of others

   My aunt Cathy is more _____gregarious_____ than my father is.

2. **mortify** *(v.)* to cause shame or humility

   My parents _____mortify_____ me when they tell stories about me as a baby.

3. **permeate** *(v.)* to spread completely throughout

   A bad mood tends to _____permeate_____ the whole group.

4. **ruminate** *(v.)* 1. to ponder; 2. to think over carefully

   They left me to _____ruminate_____ over the decision I have to make.

5. **sardonic** *(adj.)* sarcastic in a bitter or mocking way

   I did not appreciate her _____sardonic_____ response to my complaint.

Use Your Vocabulary—Challenge!

Twin Trouble Bailey and Jesse are twins, but they are nothing alike. Bailey is very talkative, while Jesse is more on the shy side. As always, they have their birthday party together, but this year they get in an argument in front of their friends. Using the five Challenge Words above, write a story about the party, the argument, and the resolution. Be creative!

> *Notable Quotes*
>
> "Speak to me as to thy thinkings,
> As thou dost **ruminate**, and give thy worst of thoughts
> The worst of words."
>
> —William Shakespeare (1564–1616),
> British playwright (from *Othello*)

FUN WITH WORDS

In chemistry, letters are used to represent different chemicals and elements. Equations such as the one below show how elements combine to form compounds:

$$2H_2 + O_2 = 2H_2O$$

This shows how hydrogen (H) and oxygen (O) can be combined to make water. In word chemistry, you'll see an equation like the one above. The letters in each equation combine to make a vocabulary word. A small number to the right of a letter tells you how many times that letter appears in the word. The clue next to the equation gives you a hint. For example:

$IS + E_2G$ = keeping you occupied _____ *siege*

The small 2 tells you there are two *E*'s in this vocabulary word. Determine how many letters are actually in the word. Then rearrange them and write the answer on the line. The answer to the example is *siege*.

1. $LBI + MA_2E$ = a formula for friendliness   *amiable*

2. $CAE + T_2DR$ = a solution that lessens   *detract*

3. $CIO + SD_2R$ = this won't agree with you   *discord*

4. $TRF + NE_2V$ = something enthusiastic   *fervent*

5. $OPL + NE_2V$ = to enclose something   *envelop*

6. $TNE + SUV + I_4Q$ = like people who ask questions   *inquisitive*

7. $R_4ZUY_2F - YR_3Z$ = this may make you angry   *fury*

8. $EI_3B_2 + KS_2R - EI_2SB$ = an active formula   *brisk*

WORD LIST

Read each word using the pronunciation key.

antic (an´ tik)

buoy (bōō´ ē)

credible (kred´ ə bəl)

devise (di vīz´)

discriminate (di skrim´ ə nāt)

ecology (ē kol´ ə jē)

esteem (e stēm´)

fiasco (fē as´ kō)

gale (gāl)

humble (hum´ bəl)

integral (in´ tə grəl)

liable (lī´ ə bəl)

mythical (mith´ i kəl)

paragon (pâr´ ə gon)

preliminary (pri lim´ ə nâr ē)

reliability (ri lī ə bil´ i tē)

silhouette (sil ōō et´)

succumb (sə kum´)

tycoon (tī kōōn´)

yarn (yärn)

WORD STUDY

Prefixes

The prefix *extra-* means "outside of" or "beyond."

extract (ek strakt´) *(v.)* to pull or draw out, often with special effort

extracurricular (ek strə kə rik´ yə lər) *(adj.)* outside of normal classwork

extradite (ek´ strə dīt) *(v.)* to give up an alleged criminal to another state or authority

extraneous (ek strā´ nē əs) *(adj.)* not relevant

extraordinary (ek strôr´ dən er ē) *(adj.)* out of the ordinary

extravagant (ek strav´ ə gənt) *(adj.)* more than is necessary

Challenge Words

accolade (ak´ ə lād)

desultory (des´ əl tôr ē)

exorbitant (ig zôr´ bi tənt)

novice (näv´ is)

pinnacle (pin´ ə kəl)

■ **TEACHER TIP:** See page ix for suggestions on how to use this page.

Read each sentence below to figure out the meaning of the word in **bold**. Use reasoning skills and the remainder of the sentence to help you. Write the meaning of the word on the line.

1. I have great **esteem** for those who volunteer at the homeless shelter.

respect or admiration

2. After the birthday cake fell on the floor, I knew that the party would be a **fiasco**.

a complete failure

3. The **gale** ripped the umbrella from my hands and tore the leaves from the trees.

a very strong, powerful wind

4. The runners competed in a **preliminary** race before proceeding to the finals.

coming before the main part; introductory

5. Sue is a **credible** witness; I believe her account of the accident.

believable; trustworthy

6. Dennis is always getting in trouble for some **antic**, such as putting bubble bath in the town fountain.

a foolish act or prank

7. Grandma is in the kitchen telling Nicky a **yarn** about her days in the army.

a story of incredible adventure

8. She had decorated the tapestry with giants, dragons, and other **mythical** creatures.

having to do with traditional stories about spirits, ancestors, or heroes

9. If you break the window, you will be **liable** for the cost of replacing it.

responsible for, according to law

10. My Uncle Leon is a well-known **tycoon** in the athletic-shoe industry.

a wealthy or powerful businessperson

WORD MEANINGS

Word Learning

Study the spelling, part(s) of speech, and meaning(s) of each word. Complete each sentence by writing the word on the line. Then read the sentence.

1. **antic** *(n.)* a foolish act or prank

   What _____antic_____ are you up to now?

2. **buoy** *(n.)* a floating device used in water as a marker or warning

   Be sure you don't swim past the _____buoy_____.

3. **credible** *(adj.)* 1. believable; trustworthy, 2. reliable

   Forgetting your homework is not a _____credible_____ excuse.

4. **devise** *(v.)* 1. to plan; 2. to invent

   They will _____devise_____ a plan to get him out of the dungeon.

5. **discriminate** *(v.)* 1. to distinguish between; 2. to observe a difference; 3. to show prejudice

   A young child often cannot _____discriminate_____ between a helpful stranger and a dangerous one.

6. **ecology** *(n.)* the study of the relationship between living things and their environment

   If you knew anything about _____ecology_____, you would not throw your garbage in that stream.

7. **esteem** *(v.)* 1. to think of with respect; 2. to consider valuable; *(n.)* respect or admiration

   We all _____esteem_____ the judge and her wise decisions.

   I hold my parents in great _____esteem_____.

8. **fiasco** *(n.)* a complete failure

   If the new cabinet falls apart, we'll have a complete _____fiasco_____ on our hands.

9. **gale** *(n.)* a very strong, powerful wind

   The little straw house could not resist the great _____gale_____.

10. **humble** *(adj.)* modest; not overly proud of one's own accomplishments; *(v.)* to humiliate or destroy the pride of

    The _____humble_____ princess never tried to promote herself.

    A defeat after so many successes would really _____humble_____ him.

155

11. **integral** *(adj.)* necessary to make a whole

A goalie is _____integral_____ to every soccer team.

12. **liable** *(adj.)* responsible for, according to law

We are _____liable_____ to pay for the damages caused by the accident.

13. **mythical** *(adj.)* 1. having to do with traditional stories about spirits, ancestors, or heroes; 2. imaginary

Many people have compared John F. Kennedy's presidency to the _____mythical_____ kingdom of Camelot.

14. **paragon** *(n.)* a model of excellence

My sister is hardly a _____paragon_____ of virtue.

15. **preliminary** *(adj.)* coming before the main part; introductory; *(n.)* a statement or action that comes before others

We should start with a _____preliminary_____ discussion of what we plan to do.

The introduction of the speaker is an important _____preliminary_____.

16. **reliability** *(n.)* dependability; the ability to be counted on

I am not too sure of the _____reliability_____ of that car.

17. **silhouette** *(n.)* the outline of something; *(v.)* to show in outline

I could see the _____silhouette_____ of my mother through the window shade.

The bright lights _____silhouette_____ his head from behind.

18. **succumb** *(v.)* 1. to give in to a stronger force; 2. to die

I will not _____succumb_____ to your wishes!

19. **tycoon** *(n.)* a wealthy or powerful businessperson

He started as a clerk but grew to be an industry _____tycoon_____.

20. **yarn** *(n.)* 1. a heavy thread used for knitting and weaving; 2. a story of adventure

I used green and blue _____yarn_____ for the scarf.

Use Your Vocabulary

Choose the word from the Word List that best completes each sentence. Write the word on the line. You may use the plural form of nouns and the past tense of verbs if necessary.

Last summer, a computer industry __1__ offered to take my Scout troop out on his yacht. Mr. Hartley is very powerful and wealthy, but he has remained __2__ and selfless. He is __3__ throughout the community as a(n) __4__ of generosity.

Mr. Hartley believes that the firsthand exploration of nature is __5__ to every child's development. Our troop had been studying marine __6__, so we were excited to see this mysterious world for ourselves.

Early one sunny Saturday, we all gathered at the dock. Mr. Hartley spoke a few __7__ words of welcome. Then, using maps and a compass, he helped us __8__ our course for the day. He also demonstrated the boat's __9__ by showing us that everything was in top condition. He assigned each scout a different task and didn't __10__ against any one of us. All of our chores were equally demanding. Finally, he warned us against any __11__. Boating was serious business, he said.

By afternoon, the sky had darkened, and a strong __12__ made it difficult to steer the boat. Mr. Hartley knew he was __13__ for our safety, and we were far from the dock. He knew his boat wouldn't __14__ to the storm, but he wanted to get us to a protected area.

He steered the boat toward the mouth of a nearby cove. A bright red __15__ floated at the cove's entrance, warning us of shallow water. But he was a __16__ leader. We had complete confidence in his ability.

The cove protected us from the storm. The area had a(n) __17__ quality about it. I could imagine magical sea creatures hiding in these waters. Mr. Hartley helped us pass the time by making animal-shaped __18__ on the wall in the lantern light. He also told us great __19__ about his adventures at sea. Late in the afternoon, the storm stopped and we headed home. Mr. Hartley apologized for the __20__, but to us, the trip had been a great adventure.

1. _____tycoon_____
2. _____humble_____
3. _____esteemed_____
4. _____paragon_____
5. _____integral_____
6. _____ecology_____
7. _____preliminary_____
8. _____devise_____
9. _____reliability_____
10. _____discriminate_____
11. _____antics_____
12. _____gale_____
13. _____liable_____
14. _____succumb_____
15. _____buoy_____
16. _____credible_____
17. _____mythical_____
18. _____silhouettes_____
19. _____yarns_____
20. _____fiasco_____

SYNONYMS

Synonyms are words that have the same or nearly the same meanings.

Part 1 Choose the word from the box that is the best synonym for each group of words. Write the word on the line.

buoy	esteem	gale	liable
credible	fiasco	integral	mythical

1. gust, windstorm _____ gale

2. value, honor; regard, approval _____ esteem

3. answerable, accountable, obligated _____ liable

4. legendary, illusory, fabled _____ mythical

5. disaster, blunder, washout _____ fiasco

6. essential, needed _____ integral

7. faithful, plausible, dependable _____ credible

8. marker, beacon, signal _____ buoy

Part 2 Replace the underlined word with a word from the box that means the same or almost the same. Write your answer on the line.

tycoon	succumb	antic	paragon
humble	devise	discriminate	

9. That was nothing but a lark. _____ antic

10. We must formulate a method of transporting our products. _____ devise

11. A great building entrepreneur lives in that mansion. _____ tycoon

12. Whatever you do, don't yield to his charms. _____ succumb

13. She went on to college to become a model of scholarship. _____ paragon

14. In the museum business, one must be able to distinguish between real and counterfeit paintings. _____ discriminate

15. Martin cast a modest glance in our direction. _____ humble

ANTONYMS

Antonyms are words that have opposite or nearly opposite meanings.

Part 1 Choose the word from the box that is the best antonym for each group of words. Write the word on the line.

humble	liable	mythical	reliability	succumb

1. real, actual, factual   *mythical*

2. proud, conceited; praise, glorify   *humble*

3. exempt, unaccountable, not responsible   *liable*

4. resist, fight, survive, live   *succumb*

5. unworthiness, instability   *reliability*

Part 2 Replace the underlined word with a word from the box that means the opposite or almost the opposite. Write your answer on the line.

esteem	fiasco	credible	integral	preliminary

6. He presented a great deal of <u>unreliable</u> evidence to the jury.   *credible*

7. I hold artists and musicians in great <u>contempt</u>.   *esteem*

8. Our swim team won the <u>final</u> race.   *preliminary*

9. Yvonne provided us with many ideas <u>unnecessary</u> to the project.

     integral

10. The carnival was a great <u>success</u>.   *fiasco*

> ## Vocabulary in Action
>
> The word **mythical** can be traced to about 1678. Its root is from the Greek *mythos*—"speech, thought, story, myth." According to the *Dictionary of English Folklore*, myths are "stories about divine beings, generally arranged in a coherent system; they are revered as true and sacred; they are endorsed by rulers and priests; and closely linked to religion. Once this link is broken, and the actors in the story are not regarded as gods but as human heroes, giants or fairies, it is no longer a myth but a folktale. Where the central actor is divine but the story is trivial . . . the result is religious legend, not myth." (p. 254)

WORD STUDY

Prefixes Choose the word from the box that best completes each of the following sentences.

extract	extradite	extraordinary
extracurricular	extraneous	extravagant

1. Her parents could not afford to support her _____extravagant_____ taste in clothing.

2. She may be small, but she possesses _____extraordinary_____ strength.

3. Just tell me the basic story; you can leave out _____extraneous_____ details.

4. The United States agreed to _____extradite_____ the German war criminal.

5. How will you ever _____extract_____ yourself from that terrible situation?

6. He keeps very busy with all of his _____extracurricular_____ activities.

Vocabulary in Action

Did you know that **extracurricular** activities first made their appearance in American colleges in the 19th century? The first extracurricular activities were student literary societies, or debate clubs. By the middle of the century, Greek fraternities and sororities emerged. Students also initiated and organized the early athletic programs at American colleges.

By the start of the 20th century, literary societies were on the decline, and some educators felt that less desirable extracurricular activities were now distracting students from their curricular responsibilities. Intercollegiate athletics soon became the dominant element in the extracurriculum in most American colleges and high schools. Such activities as school newspapers and interschool sports programs have been part of American high schools since the World War I era.

CHALLENGE WORDS

Word Learning—Challenge!

Study the spelling, part of speech, and meaning(s) of each word. Complete each sentence by writing the word on the line. Then read the sentence.

1. **accolade** (*n.*) something given as a sign of approval, praise, or respect

    Her smile and thanks were _____accolade_____ enough for me.

2. **desultory** (*adj.*) 1. lacking planning, order, or purpose; 2. random

    We spent the afternoon in _____desultory_____ conversation.

3. **exorbitant** (*adj.*) 1. exceeding in intensity or quality; 2. too much

    They have spent _____exorbitant_____ amounts of money fixing the kitchen.

4. **novice** (*n.*) a beginner; someone new at something

    Bill is really a _____novice_____ at sailing.

5. **pinnacle** (*n.*) 1. a high peak; 2. a pointed top, as of a mountain

    At the _____pinnacle_____ of his career, he played the role of Hamlet.

Use Your Vocabulary—Challenge!

Award Speech The time has come to award the Great Big Prize to the citizen who has contributed the most to the well-being of the children of your community. Using the five Challenge Words above, write a speech awarding this year's Great Big Prize to a real or an imaginary person.

> ### Vocabulary in Action
>
> The word **desultory** (ca. 1581) comes from the Latin word *desultorius*. This is the adjective form of *desultur,* which means "hasty, casual, superficial." The word's noun form refers to "a rider in the circus who jumped from one horse to another while they are in gallop."

Ten vocabulary words are hidden in the puzzle below. Words may appear backward, forward, up, down, or diagonally. Find and circle all the words.

```
I M L U C M N Y T T R I L I G E
J C G N I O G O Z O H T F F W S
A I T H O R E F Y G O L O C E I
C P D C E G S N D N T O F I M M
K O Y A T D A O O B A Y M E O O
L T A K E E L R N S H V U E X R
Y E N L F R S C A I U U T G N V
T L V A O H A E S P M C I F O K
O A J C S A N Q R R B T C I R E
A Z E I U R T A O K L E H U S X
N Z O H R C V B Q A E L G I M O
T E J T D L O O Y C J M O B I B
I B C Y B O G I E S I V E D T L
C N U M V A R N C K O A I E L E
I E E X L R E F I A S C O D D H
Z B L E Z I S Y L B A I N E L S
```

Vocabulary in Action

Tycoon and *love* are two words not often associated with one another. But F. Scott Fitzgerald wrote a novel titled *The Love of The Last Tycoon*. The novel centers on the life of Hollywood film executive Monroe Stahr in the 1930s. Stahr's character is very loosely modeled on the life of film executive Irving Thalberg. Fitzgerald died suddenly, at age 45, leaving the book unfinished. The notes for the novel were collected and edited by literary critic Edmund Wilson, who was a close friend of Fitzgerald's. The unfinished novel was originally published in 1941 under the title *The Last Tycoon*.

WORD LIST

Read each word using the pronunciation key.

antithesis (an tith´ ə sis)

burly (bər´ lē)

crucial (krōō´ shəl)

devote (di vōt´)

disentangle (dis in taŋ´ gəl)

economic (e kə nom´ ic)

ethnic (eth´ nik)

fidelity (fi del´ i tē)

garish (gâr´ ish)

hurdle (hər´ dəl)

intervene (in tər vēn´)

literacy (lit´ ər ə sē)

naive (nī ēv´)

perimeter (pə rim´ i tər)

presumptuous (pri zump´ chōō əs)

reminisce (rem ə nis´)

siphon (sī´ fən)

sustain (sə stān´)

ultimate (ul´ tə mət)

zeal (zēl)

WORD STUDY

Analogies

Analogies show relationships between pairs of words. Study the relationships between the pairs of words below.

backpack is to **student** as **briefcase** is to **lawyer**

biology is to **doctor** as **math** is to **accountant**

lion is to **Africa** as **panda** is to **Asia**

Challenge Words

abhor (ab hôr´)

discernible (di sərn´ ə bəl)

effrontery (e frunt´ ər ē)

finagle (fə nā´ gəl)

precipice (pres´ i pis)

■ **TEACHER TIP:** See page ix for suggestions on how to use this page.

Level H

Read each sentence below to figure out the meaning of the word in **bold**. Use reasoning skills and the remainder of the sentence to help you. Write the meaning of the word on the line.

1. Should we **intervene** or let the group work out the problem on its own?

   to come between; to interfere

2. A metal fence ran along the **perimeter** of the park.

   the edge around a space

3. Good weather is **crucial** for the launching of the space shuttle.

   vitally important or essential

4. Martina cleaned the chalkboard with such **zeal** that her teacher let her do it daily.

   eager attention or enthusiasm for a cause or goal

5. The town has severe **economic** problems; several businesses have closed in the last two months.

   having to do with the management and behavior of goods, services, and money

6. After law school, Patricia's **ultimate** goal is to become a Supreme Court justice.

   of the greatest size or importance

7. One bowl of cereal will not **sustain** a growing child for a whole day.

   to provide for

8. The principal said that Kevin's yellow and purple suit was too **garish** to wear at graduation.

   having excessively bright colors or decorations; gaudy

9. People value dogs as pets because of their **fidelity** to their owners.

   loyalty

10. I never thought she would be so **presumptuous** as to fix herself a sandwich in someone else's house.

    inappropriately bold or confident

WORD MEANINGS

Word Learning

Study the spelling, part(s) of speech, and meaning(s) of each word. Complete each sentence by writing the word on the line. Then read the sentence.

1. **antithesis** *(n.)* the direct opposite

   Her idea is the _____ antithesis _____ of everything we've worked for.

2. **burly** *(adj.)* 1. large in bodily size; 2. strongly built; 3. stout

   We found a _____ burly _____ police officer to help us lift the fallen tree.

3. **crucial** *(adj.)* vitally important or essential

   You have forgotten one _____ crucial _____ point.

4. **devote** *(v.)* 1. to apply entirely to one activity; 2. to set aside for some purpose

   Jeb decided to _____ devote _____ all of his free time to practicing his tennis game.

5. **disentangle** *(v.)* to free from entanglement or complication

   The turtle tried to _____ disentangle _____ itself from the fishing net.

6. **economic** *(adj.)* having to do with the management and behavior of goods, services, and money

   The country has reached an _____ economic _____ crisis.

7. **ethnic** *(adj.)* of a particular religious, racial, national, or cultural group

   You'll find a number of _____ ethnic _____ restaurants on Macomb Street.

8. **fidelity** *(n.)* 1. loyalty; 2. faithfulness to obligations

   His employers valued his _____ fidelity _____ to the company.

9. **garish** *(adj.)* having excessively bright colors or decorations, gaudy

   I don't much care for that _____ garish _____ window display.

10. **hurdle** *(n.)* 1. a barrier used in foot races; 2. a problem that must be overcome; *(v.)* 1. to jump over a barrier; 2. to overcome a problem

    Mark's brother cut his leg on a racing _____ hurdle _____.

    We watched the children _____ hurdle _____ the fence.

11. **intervene** *(v.)* 1. to come between; to interfere; 2. to happen between two points of time

    I didn't intend to _____ intervene _____, so I'll leave you two alone now.

12. **literacy** *(n.)* the ability to read and write

Compared with many countries, the United States has a high rate of
_____literacy_____.

13. **naive** *(adj.)* 1. showing great simplicity; 2. without much knowledge of the world

You say she's lived all over the world, but she appears so _____naive_____.

14. **perimeter** *(n.)* 1. the edge around a space; 2. the length of the edge around a space

We planted daffodils and tulips around the _____perimeter_____ of the yard.

15. **presumptuous** *(adj.)* inappropriately bold or confident

Would it be _____presumptuous_____ of me to ask for a raise?

16. **reminisce** *(v.)* to remember or talk about past events

My mom likes to visit with her sisters and _____reminisce_____ about their childhood.

17. **siphon** *(n.)* a curved pipe or tube used to move a liquid from one container to another; *(v.)* to take out by using a siphon

You'll have to use a _____siphon_____ to drain the tank.

A long tube will _____siphon_____ water from the basin.

18. **sustain** *(v.)* 1. to keep; to prolong; 2. to provide for

I can't _____sustain_____ this effort much longer.

19. **ultimate** *(adj.)* 1. final; 2. of the greatest size or importance; *(n.)* 1. the final point; 2. the greatest point

At the top of the hill, she faced the _____ultimate_____ challenge.

As an athlete, she strove for the _____ultimate_____.

20. **zeal** *(n.)* eager attention or enthusiasm for a cause or goal

Lucas could not contain his _____zeal_____ for writing stories.

Vocabulary in Action

The word **antithesis** (ca. 1529) comes from the Late Latin word *antithesis* (Greek "antithesis" or "opposition"). It literally means "a placing against."

Use Your Vocabulary

Choose the word from the Word List that best completes each sentence. Write the word on the line. You may use the plural form of nouns and the past tense of verbs if necessary.

Although the program had overcome other difficulties, Books Across Borders now faced its greatest __1__ ever. The organization worked to raise the level of __2__ across all __3__ groups and neighborhood lines in the city of Little Falls. Its __4__ to community values and sound teaching had earned it a very good reputation. Books Across Borders had volunteers who __5__ every weekend to distributing books and tutoring children and adults. These volunteers applied themselves to the task with __6__; they represented the __7__ of selfish city dwellers.

However, Joyce Balderas, the organization's leader, found that Books Across Borders faced serious __8__ trouble. A local company, which had always contributed a(n) __9__ portion of the group's annual budget, had just closed. Joyce was not so __10__ to think that enthusiasm alone would __11__ the organization.

Joyce walked around the __12__ of her tiny office, thinking of how to __13__ Books Across Borders from this financial trap. She hoped she would not have to __14__ money away from the tutorial programs in order to pay the rent. She __15__ aloud about the old days, when the organization did not even have an office but worked out of her dining room. Could they do without an office again?

Someone knocked on the door. She opened it to a __16__ man dressed in __17__ clothing.

"I don't mean to be __18__, he said, "but I overheard you talking to yourself and I think I may have the __19__ answer to your problems." He said that he knew of several small companies that wanted to donate to the organization.

"Thank you so much!" Joyce said. "You have __20__ just in time!"

1. _____ hurdle
2. _____ literacy
3. _____ ethnic
4. _____ fidelity
5. _____ devoted
6. _____ zeal
7. _____ antithesis
8. _____ economic
9. _____ crucial
10. _____ naive
11. _____ sustain
12. _____ perimeter
13. _____ disentangle
14. _____ siphon
15. _____ reminisced
16. _____ burly
17. _____ garish
18. _____ presumptuous
19. _____ ultimate
20. _____ intervened

SYNONYMS

Synonyms are words that have the same or nearly the same meanings.

Part 1 Choose the word from the box that is the best synonym for each group of words. Write the word on the line.

burly	intervene	presumptuous	sustain
crucial	perimeter	reminisce	ultimate

1. recollect, remember   _____reminisce_____

2. maintain, nurture, support   _____sustain_____

3. border, circumference, boundary   _____perimeter_____

4. last, conclusive, utmost, peak   _____ultimate_____

5. bold, overconfident, impertinent   _____presumptuous_____

6. step in, mediate, intercede   _____intervene_____

7. critical, significant, momentous   _____crucial_____

8. brawny, stocky, hefty   _____burly_____

Part 2 Replace the underlined word with a word from the box that means the same or almost the same. Write your answer on the line.

garish	antithesis	hurdle	naive
ethnic	fidelity	zeal	

9. She performed the role with great <u>fervor</u>. _____zeal_____

10. People of many different <u>national</u> groups lived in the neighborhood.
_____ethnic_____

11. Jasmine knew that to become senator she'd have to overcome a great <u>obstacle</u>.
_____hurdle_____

12. The two have always shown great <u>allegiance</u> to each other. _____fidelity_____

13. We are striving not for war but for its <u>opposite</u>. _____antithesis_____

14. Scott has a very <u>innocent</u> view of the world. _____naive_____

15. Whenever we have a party, Erika shows up in <u>flashy</u> clothing.

_____garish_____

ANTONYMS

Antonyms are words that have opposite or nearly opposite meanings.

Part 1 Choose the word from the box that is the best antonym for each group of words. Write the word on the line.

antithesis	fidelity	presumptuous
disentangle	perimeter	sustain

1. twin, equal, duplicate _____antithesis_____

2. hesitant, insecure, unsure _____presumptuous_____

3. snare, catch, tie up _____disentangle_____

4. center, middle, core _____perimeter_____

5. discontinue, stop, let down _____sustain_____

6. falseness, treason, fickleness _____fidelity_____

Part 2 Replace the underlined word with a word from the box that means the opposite or almost the opposite. Write your answer on the line.

garish	crucial	zeal
naive	burly	ultimate

7. Look at those <u>puny</u> arms! _____burly_____

8. The substitute teacher appears to be very <u>sophisticated</u>. _____naive_____

9. You have forgotten a few <u>trivial</u> details. _____crucial_____

10. She wore a <u>plain</u> scarf around her neck. _____garish_____

11. My <u>initial</u> goal is to finish this assignment on time. _____ultimate_____

12. Hunter responded to every request with <u>indifference</u>. _____zeal_____

WORD STUDY

Analogies To complete the following analogies, decide what kind of relationship is shown by the first pair of words. Then fill in the bubble next to the other pair of words that show the same relationship.

1. **big** is to **enormous** as
   - a. little is to huge
   - **b. small is to tiny**
   - c. right is to wrong
   - d. delicious is to sweet

2. **bulldozer** is to **construction** as
   - **a. submarine is to war**
   - b. hammer is to nail
   - c. horse is to training
   - d. ship is to sailor

3. **winter** is to **shiver** as
   - a. autumn is to sleep
   - b. night is to watch
   - c. evening is to follow
   - **d. summer is to sweat**

4. **curtain** is to **window** as
   - **a. sheet is to bed**
   - b. water is to faucet
   - c. melon is to knife
   - d. napkin is to crumb

5. **tooth** is to **comb** as
   - a. sand is to water
   - **b. brick is to wall**
   - c. paper is to computer
   - d. TV is to library

6. **apple** is to **fruit** as
   - a. fish is to fowl
   - b. ice cream is to milk
   - **c. perch is to fish**
   - d. tree is to oak

Vocabulary in Action

Many scientists believe that analogy plays a major role in problem solving, decision making, memory, creativity, emotion, and communication. Analogy lies behind basic tasks such as the identification of places, objects, and people. In fact, some scientists have argued that analogy is "the core of cognition."

CHALLENGE WORDS

Word Learning—Challenge!

Study the spelling, part of speech, and meaning of each word. Complete each sentence by writing the word on the line. Then read the sentence.

1. **abhor** *(v.)* to feel great hatred or disgust for

   I _____ abhor _____ the practice of cheating on tests.

2. **discernible** *(adj.)* able to be seen or perceived

   Her footprints were barely _____ discernible _____ in the drifting snow.

3. **effrontery** *(n.)* audacity; boldness

   I thought he showed great _____ effrontery _____ in speaking to his elders that way.

4. **finagle** *(v.)* to get something by being tricky or clever

   Julia managed to _____ finagle _____ a couple of tickets to the game.

5. **precipice** *(n.)* a very steep cliff or overhanging place

   One lone bush grew atop the _____ precipice _____.

Use Your Vocabulary—Challenge!

Librarian's Lament You are a librarian at a local library. While you love books and working with people, you sometimes feel frustrated by patrons who show disrespect for the library, its books, or other patrons. Using the five Challenge Words above, write a diary entry explaining how you feel about your job.

Notable Quotes

"Most are engaged in business the greater part of their lives, because the soul **abhors** a vacuum and they have not discovered any continuous employment for man's nobler faculties."

—Henry David Thoreau (1817–1862), American writer and philosopher

FUN WITH WORDS

You've just been hired by a local artist to name her new paintings. Below you'll find a description of each painting and a partial title. Fill in the blank in each title with the vocabulary word from this chapter that fits best.

1. This painting shows two boys using a tube to drain water from one bathtub to another. It's entitled "The _____Siphon_____."

2. The canvas of this painting is composed entirely of one-dollar bills. Name this one "A(n) _____Economic_____ Foundation."

3. Only the outer edges of this piece have been painted. It's called "Living on the _____Perimeter_____."

4. In this work, three flies try to save another fly who is caught in a spiderweb. Its title is "Hoping to _____Disentangle_____ a Friend."

5. Two people are on a porch swing, watching the sunset and looking through an old photograph album. This painting's name is "A Good Time to _____Reminisce_____."

6. Half of this painting is white, while the other half is completely black. Call this one "_____Antithesis_____."

7. This painting shows two men standing together. Both men are more than 7 feet tall and each weighs nearly 300 pounds. It's called "The _____Burly_____ Brothers."

8. In this painting, two children are holding the earth gently in their hands. Call it "Let's _____Sustain_____ Our World."

NAME _____

Review 13–15

Word Meanings Fill in the bubble of the word that is best defined by each phrase.

1. to mangle or disable
   a. reiterate   **b. mutilate**   c. oscillate   d. discriminate

2. a silly act or caper
   a. controversy   b. paragon   c. siphon   **d. antic**

3. capable of being read
   a. legible   b. crucial   c. burly   d. durable

4. the maximum
   a. reliability   **b. ultimate**   c. gale   d. subordination

5. showing great emotion
   a. ethnic   b. inquisitive   **c. fervent**   d. ultimate

6. to regard or value highly
   a. succumb   b. envelop   c. devote   **d. esteem**

7. overly bright or ornamented
   a. brisk   b. mythical   **c. garish**   d. naive

8. the blockade of a town or fortress
   a. siege   b. fiasco   c. perimeter   d. fury

9. a complete opposite
   a. zeal   b. integral   c. fidelity   **d. antithesis**

10. capable of withstanding wear and tear
    a. humble   **b. durable**   c. credible   d. amiable

11. a perfect example
    a. paragon   b. buoy   c. predator   d. tycoon

12. to supply with needed nourishment
    a. sustain   b. devise   c. detract   d. devote

13. heavy and strong
    a. liable   b. fervent   **c. burly**   d. wretched

14. an adventure tale
    a. yarn   b. siege   c. fiasco   d. hurdle

15. to recall the past
    a. reminisce   b. disentangle   c. envelop   d. intervene

16. contempt or aggressive dislike
    a. ecology   b. antic   c. literacy   **d. hostility**

Level H   Review 13–15

17. legally obligated

    (**a.**)presumptuous   (**b.**)liable   **c.** inquisitive   **d.** ethnic

18. of the highest importance

    (**a.**)garish   (**b.**)crucial   **c.** brisk   (**d.**)preliminary

19. lack of harmony

    (**a.**)twinge   (**b.**)reliability   **c.** silhouette   (**d.**)discord

20. worthy of confidence

    (**a.**)economic   (**b.**)naive   (**c.**)credible   (**d.**)legible

Sentence Completion
Choose the word from the box that best completes each of the following sentences. Write the word in the blank.

fiasco	oscillates	amiable	tycoon	silhouettes
succumb	presumptuous	humble	gale	siphon

1. After oil was discovered on his farm, Jake became a petroleum _____tycoon_____ almost overnight.

2. We bought a fan that _____oscillates_____ on its base and blows air all across the room.

3. My father and I were able to _____siphon_____ some gas from the car's tank into the lawn mower's tank.

4. Light from the candle cast eerie, flickering _____silhouettes_____ of us onto the far wall.

5. The _____presumptuous_____ senior was shocked to learn that he had not been elected homecoming king.

6. We knew that the play was a complete _____fiasco_____ when two of the props collapsed.

7. Even though she's now an international star, Katelyn has remained as _____humble_____ as ever.

8. We hope our parents _____succumb_____ to our pleas to let us go to the beach.

9. Spending time with friends always puts me in a(n) _____amiable_____ mood.

10. We secured the windows when the _____gale_____ began to grow stronger.

Fill in the Blanks
Fill in the bubble of the pair of words that best completes each sentence.

1. The old sailor spun a(n) ____ about a ____ sea monster from an ancient legend.
   - **a.** fury, wretched
   - **b.** yarn, mythical
   - **c.** antic, garish
   - **d.** controversy, durable

2. Chuck had to ____ the ____ kitten from the vine it tried to climb.
   - **a.** disentangle, inquisitive
   - **b.** oscillate, legible
   - **c.** reminisce, mythical
   - **d.** detract, brisk

3. The ____ draft of my story is barely ____.
   - **a.** burly, presumptuous
   - **b.** crucial, humble
   - **c.** garish, mythical
   - **d.** preliminary, legible

4. My little sister is so ____ that she thinks that anything I tell her is ____.
   - **a.** naive, credible
   - **b.** burly, presumptuous
   - **c.** durable, crucial
   - **d.** fervent, economic

5. The volunteer's ____ for the cause makes her our most ____ worker.
   - **a.** siphon, mythical
   - **b.** twinge, inquisitive
   - **c.** zeal, fervent
   - **d.** perimeter, ultimate

6. The ____ between the two former best friends was so strong that their teacher felt she had to ____.
   - **a.** fidelity, discriminate
   - **b.** discord, intervene
   - **c.** buoy, detract
   - **d.** silhouette, reiterate

7. Gerry has overcome so many ____ that everyone holds her in high ____.
   - **a.** paragons, humble
   - **b.** predators, siege
   - **c.** tycoons, literacy
   - **d.** hurdles, esteem

8. The party turned into a(n) ____ after two guests displayed their ____.
   - **a.** antithesis, buoys
   - **b.** ecology, literacy
   - **c.** hurdle, reliability
   - **d.** fiasco, hostility

9. The club members gathered to ____ a plan to better their ____ situation by doing odd jobs.
   - **a.** devise, economic
   - **b.** mutilate, amiable
   - **c.** oscillate, integral
   - **d.** envelop, brisk

10. The clown's ____ costume is the ____ of beautiful.
   - **a.** wretched, tycoon
   - **b.** garish, antithesis
   - **c.** liable, ultimate
   - **d.** mythical, subordination

Classifying Words
Sort the words in the box by writing each word to complete a phrase in the correct category.

amiable	controversy	devoted	disentangle	durable
envelops	ethnic	fidelity	garish	hostility
humble	mutilated	perimeter	reliability	reminisce
succumbs	sustained	twinge	wretched	zeal

Words You Might Use to Talk About Moods

1. cheerful and _____ amiable _____ every day

2. always so _____ humble _____ even though she is very talented

3. scowling face makes him seem filled with _____ hostility _____

4. dives into every project with energy and _____ zeal _____

5. never _____ succumbs _____ to unhappiness

Words You Might Use to Talk About Friendship

6. sympathy that _____ sustained _____ her the day her dog died

7. proves his _____ fidelity _____ by keeping my secrets

8. can always be counted on for honesty and _____ reliability _____

9. _____ devoted _____ to everyone who has been kind to her

10. likes to _____ reminisce _____ about our kindergarten days

Words You Might Use to Talk About Things That Go Wrong

11. a(n) _____ twinge _____ in my back from picking up the heavy suitcase

12. baby sister who _____ mutilated _____ her brother's science report

13. _____ controversy _____ with Dad about cleaning our room

14. stop to _____ disentangle _____ my hair from the bubble gum

15. feeling _____ wretched _____ because he has the flu

Words You Might Use to Talk About Clothing

16. favorite _____ ethnic _____ costume for family holidays

17. fringe around the _____ perimeter _____ of the hat's brim

18. comfortable, long-lasting, _____ durable _____ jeans

19. a(n) _____ garish _____ shirt with a big print in bright colors

20. hood that _____ envelops _____ my ears on cold days

Posttest

Choosing the Definitions Fill in the bubble next to the item that best defines the boldface word in each sentence.

Ch. 6   1. The babysitter takes Lulu for a daily **jaunt** to the park.
     (a.) jog   (**b.**) outing   (c.) ride   (d.) gate

Ch. 8   2. Computers quickly become obsolete.
     (**a.**) out-of-date   (b.) powerful   (c.) enjoyable   (d.) up-to-date

Ch. 10   3. The police spotted the **fugitive** in front of the abandoned building.
     (a.) older woman   (b.) stolen goods   (c.) car   (**d.**) runaway

Ch. 15   4. The next week we all got together to **reminisce** about the dance.
     (a.) wonder   (b.) forget   (c.) guess   (**d.**) remember

Ch. 9   5. Some people blush and **stammer** when they are nervous.
     (a.) perspire   (b.) fidget   (**c.**) stutter   (d.) relax

Ch. 8   6. The absolute **minimum** Justin will sell the bike for is $20.
     (a.) most   (**b.**) least   (c.) price   (d.) deal

Ch. 12   7. Don't drink from that cup with a chip in its **brim**.
     (a.) bottom   (b.) handle   (**c.**) **edge**   (d.) design

Ch. 7   8. When the rescuers found the lost child, she was suffering from **dehydration**.
     (**a.**) lack of water   (b.) lack of air   (c.) extreme heat   (d.) extreme cold

Ch. 10   9. The forest ranger lives as a **recluse** for part of the year.
     (a.) mountaineer   (**b.**) hermit   (c.) pioneer   (d.) firefighter

Ch. 14   10. In the flickering light, I saw a strange **silhouette** on the wall.
     (a.) painting   (**b.**) shadow   (c.) stain   (d.) curtain

Ch. 15   11. That rude attitude is the **antithesis** of friendliness.
     (a.) beginning   (b.) example   (**c.**) opposite   (d.) offspring

Ch. 7   12. William Shakespeare achieved **immortality** through his plays.
     (**a.**) lasting fame (b.) beautiful poetry (c.) large audiences (d.) great wealth

Ch. 2   13. Jocelyn had an **absurd** idea for a gift for our father.
     (a.) brilliant   (b.) unique   (c.) reasonable   (**d.**) foolish

Ch. 3   14. We won't give up until we've **exhausted** all our options.
     (a.) considered   (b.) counted   (**c.**) used up   (d.) acted on

Ch. 2   15. Paul acts as if losing the game is a huge **calamity**.
     (a.) victory   (**b.**) disaster   (c.) disappointment (d.) score

177

Ch. 1 16. Cats have a reputation for being **finicky** eaters.
　　(a.) picky　　　(b.) gluttonous　　(c.) frequent　　(d.) quiet

Ch. 11 17. Before Stephen chose his new car, he **agonized** about the decision for weeks.
　　(a.) worried　　(b.) thought　　　(c.) cried　　　(d.) read

Ch. 11 18. The **drone** of the air conditioner put Alora to sleep.
　　(a.) cool air　　(b.) clanking　　(c.) breaking down　(d.) hum

Ch. 5 19. The volunteers **itemized** the supplies to go in each kit.
　　(a.) arranged　　(b.) listed　　　(c.) distributed　　(d.) hid

Ch. 6 20. Julian's answer wasn't brilliant, but it was an **admissible** response.
　　(a.) bold　　　(b.) uncertain　　(c.) incorrect　　(d.) acceptable

Ch. 4 21. Accuracy on the test is more important than speed.
　　(a.) thinking　　(b.) handwriting　(c.) correctness　(d.) attitude

Ch. 9 22. If we sit on the **knoll**, we'll have a view of the whole park.
　　(a.) stool　　　(b.) ground　　(c.) hill　　　(d.) ledge

Ch. 12 23. The group met to decide how to **allocate** the money the car wash raised.
　　(a.) distribute　　(b.) spend　　(c.) invest　　(d.) count

Ch. 10 24. On every holiday, our family gets together for a **bounteous** meal.
　　(a.) spicy　　　(b.) plentiful　　(c.) delicious　　(d.) shared

Ch. 3 25. Cracking her knuckles is my cousin's most annoying **quirk**.
　　(a.) noise　　　(b.) feeling　　(c.) pest　　　(d.) habit

Ch. 5 26. Ethan is fascinated by musicians, painters, and others of that **ilk**.
　　(a.) origin　　　(b.) type　　　(c.) opinion　　(d.) belief

Ch. 9 27. The first football practice was a real **fiasco**.
　　(a.) comedy　　(b.) success　　(c.) failure　　(d.) party

Ch. 11 28. I planted a **multitude** of flowers, but only a few came up.
　　(a.) variety　　(b.) garden　　(c.) bouquet　　(d.) vast number

Ch. 12 29. Jordan never had an **inkling** that her friends were planning a surprise party.
　　(a.) doubt　　　(b.) concern　　(c.) hint　　　(d.) reminder

Ch. 14 30. Which candidate do you plan to **endorse**?
　　(a.) watch　　　(b.) approve　　(c.) vote for　　(d.) campaign
　　　　　　　　　　　　　　　　　　　　　　　　　　　against

Word Relations

Synonyms are words that have the same or nearly the same meanings. Antonyms are words that have the opposite or nearly the opposite meanings. In the blank before each pair of words, write *S* if the words are synonyms, *A* if they are antonyms, or *N* if they are not related.

1. __N__ fluted   sedate
2. __A__ emotional   stoic
3. __N__ inquisitive   unintelligible
4. __N__ controversy   siege
5. __N__ aspiration   sequence
6. __N__ upkeep   upheaval
7. __A__ squelch   sustain
8. __S__ laud   esteem
9. __N__ isolate   secrete
10. __S__ pivot   oscillate
11. __A__ dismay   jollity
12. __S__ facet   component
13. __A__ tranquil   irascible
14. __N__ endeavor   subordination
15. __A__ burly   gaunt

16. __A__ afflicted   indifferent
17. __N__ detract   exert
18. __S__ crucial   fundamental
19. __N__ frail   tangible
20. __S__ fury   tumult
21. __S__ fatigued   weary
22. __A__ amiable   belligerent
23. __N__ optical   opaque
24. __A__ benign   ferocious
25. __S__ catastrophe calamity
26. __S__ jaunt   excursion
27. __N__ lithe   luminous
28. __A__ inadequate   admissible
29. __N__ finite   fiasco
30. __S__ agitate   stimulate

Using Context Clues

Fill in the bubble next to the phrase that best completes each sentence.

Ch. 5 1. Savannah hoped the man was **acquitted** because
    (a.) she believed he was innocent. (c.) she believed he was guilty.
    (b.) he didn't like his job. (d.) she wanted his job.

Ch. 15 2. **Literacy** is important when you are
    (a.) eating dinner. (c.) doing someone a favor.
    (b.) exercising. (d.) filling out a job application.

Ch. 7 3. Tom **endeared** himself to Jenny by
    (a.) being kind to her. (c.) avoiding her.
    (b.) ridiculing her. (d.) moving next door to her.

Ch. 4 **4.** A **pillar** is usually used to
- a. remove skin from a vegetable.
- b. support a roof.
- c. remove a splinter.
- d. take a nap.

Ch. 6 **5.** If you have **tenacity**, you have
- a. flexibility.
- b. fear.
- c. determination.
- d. an upset stomach.

Ch. 1 **6.** Those who **persist** in a task
- a. will never finish it.
- b. will be scolded.
- c. will most likely finish it.
- d. will be rewarded.

Ch. 14 **7.** A **buoy** is usually
- a. in the water.
- b. tied to a tree.
- c. on a mountainside.
- d. hard to see.

Ch. 5 **8.** A **rascal** is known for his or her
- a. magic tricks.
- b. seriousness.
- c. bravery.
- d. unruly behavior.

Ch. 4 **9.** Will's **elimination** from the spelling bee
- a. earned him a trophy.
- b. left only three contestants.
- c. was in Monday's newspaper.
- d. made him very proud.

Ch. 14 **10.** If you are **liable** for the damage, you
- a. are sorry for it.
- b. are angry about it.
- c. are responsible for it.
- d. have lied about it.

Ch. 15 **11.** The **ultimate** letter in the alphabet is
- a. the first one.
- b. the most common one.
- c. the least common one.
- d. the last one.

Ch. 15 **12.** Elena has **devoted** herself to the project because she
- a. doesn't have time for it.
- b. has lost interest in it.
- c. believes it is an important one.
- d. isn't sure whom she will vote for.

Ch. 2 **13.** Your argument is so **persuasive** that
- a. I have changed my mind.
- b. I can't believe what you say.
- c. nobody will listen to it.
- d. you will surely offend someone.

Ch. 3 **14.** He acted as an **accessory** to the theft by
- a. arresting the criminal.
- b. helping the thief escape.
- c. calling the police.
- d. distracting the thief.

Ch. 13 15. You may want to **envelop** the baby in a
    a. blanket.   **c.** bathtub.
    b. bonnet.   **d.** playpen.

Ch. 14 16. We questioned the car's **reliability**
    a. when we painted it.   **c.** when it wouldn't start.
    b. because it had no radio.   **d.** because we wanted to sell it.

Ch. 15 17. A person demonstrates **fidelity** by
    a. playing a musical instrument.   **c.** keeping promises.
    b. acting in a play.   **d.** breaking promises.

Ch. 13 18. Ariana took a **brisk** walk around the block because
    a. she had plenty of time.   **c.** she was recovering from an illness.
    b. she didn't have much time.   **d.** she was tired.

Ch. 12 19. You are **entitled** to enter the theater if you
    a. try to sneak in the back door.   **c.** don't like horror movies.
    b. have purchased a ticket.   **d.** have forgotten your money.

Ch. 5 20. In **defiance** of the law, Jon
    a. read a book about lawyers.   **c.** voted in every election.
    b. stopped at every red light.   **d.** sped through the stop sign.

Ch. 2 21. You may be **astounded** when
    a. a red light turns green.   **c.** your friends give you a surprise party.
    b. leaves begin to sprout in   **d.** your favorite TV show airs each week.
        the spring.

Ch. 7 22. Animals that **forage** are
    a. trotting along.   **c.** looking for a home.
    b. playing together.   **d.** searching for food.

Ch. 9 23. If you dream of leading a **monarchy**, you wish you could
    a. be a king or a queen.   **c.** be at the head of a parade.
    b. migrate with butterflies.   **d.** live the life of a recluse.

Ch. 14 24. If you are frightened by a **gale**, you are
    a. scared of a small girl.   **c.** caught in a storm.
    b. locked inside a fence.   **d.** lost at the zoo.

Ch. 11 25. An **optimistic** person
    a. has a gloomy outlook.   **c.** has a new pair of glasses.
    b. looks for good things in life.   **d.** is standing on a hill.

Analogies Analogies show relationships between pairs of words.

To complete the analogies, decide what kind of relationship is shown by the first pair of words. Then fill in the bubble next to the other pair of words that show the same relationship.

Ch. 6 **1. saline** is to **ocean** as
- (a.) punishment is to strict
- (b.) lengthy is to brief
- (c.) sour is to lemon
- (d.) caustic is to praise

Ch. 4 **2. flippant** is to **respectful** as
- (a.) harmful is to beneficial
- (b.) scholar is to studious
- (c.) average is to mediocre
- (d.) engine is to powerful

Ch. 14 **3. credible** is to **believable** as
- (a.) engaged is to occupied
- (b.) forever is to infinite
- (c.) worrisome is to problem
- (d.) persuade is to convince

Ch. 7 **4. commencement** is to **beginning** as
- (a.) queen is to monarchy
- (b.) gale is to moan
- (c.) perimeter is to boundary
- (d.) argument is to intervene

Ch. 8 **5. empty** is to **bucket** as
- (a.) conceal is to display
- (b.) scold is to compliment
- (c.) deflate is to tire
- (d.) snare is to trap

Ch. 6 **6. accident** is to **haphazard** as
- (a.) casual is to nonchalant
- (b.) lamp is to luminous
- (c.) ambitious is to lazy
- (d.) trivia is to significant

Ch. 8 **7. scrutinize** is to **skim** as
- (a.) wonder is to mystery
- (b.) decry is to criticize
- (c.) alarm is to comfort
- (d.) respond is to reply

Ch. 6 **8. squander** is to **waste** as
- (a.) savory is to meal
- (b.) stash is to spend
- (c.) splinter is to board
- (d.) plunder is to steal

Ch. 4 **9. encounter** is to **random** as
- (a.) curiosity is to knowledge
- (b.) maneuver is to skillful
- (c.) feat is to accomplishment
- (d.) bilk is to cheat

Ch. 4 **10. disown** is to **reject** as
- (a.) secure is to loosen
- (b.) charge is to drain
- (c.) free is to acquit
- (d.) grief is to mourn

Test-Taking Tips

Taking a standardized test can be tough. Here are a few things you can do to make the experience easier.

Get a good night's sleep the night before the test. You want to be alert and rested in the morning.

Eat a healthful breakfast. Your brain needs good food to work properly.

Wear layers of clothing. You can take off or put on a layer if you get too warm or too cold.

Have two sharp number 2 pencils—with erasers—ready.

When you get the test, read the directions carefully. Be sure you understand what you are supposed to do. If you have any questions, ask your teacher before you start marking your answers.

If you feel nervous, close your eyes and take a deep breath as you silently count to three. Then slowly breathe out. Do this several times until your mind is calm.

Manage your time. Check to see how many questions there are. Try to answer half the questions before half the time is up.

Answer the easy questions first. If you don't know the answer to a question, skip it and come back to it later.

Try to answer all the questions. Some will seem very hard, but don't worry about it. Nobody is expected to get every answer right. Make the best guess you can.

If you make a mistake, erase it completely. Then write the correct answer or fill in the correct circle.

When you have finished, go back over the test. Work on any questions you skipped. Check your answers.

Question Types

Many tests contain the same kinds of questions. Here are a few question types you may encounter.

Meaning from Context

This kind of question asks you to figure out the meaning of a word from the words or sentences around it.

> The smoke from the smoldering garbage made her eyes water.

Which word in the sentence helps you understand the meaning of *smoldering*?

smoke	garbage
eyes	water

Read the sentence carefully. You know that smoke comes from something that is burning. *Smoldering* must mean "burning." *Smoke* is the correct answer.

Synonyms and Antonyms

Some questions ask you to identify the synonym of a word. Synonyms are words that mean the same. Some questions ask you to identify the antonym of a word. Antonyms are words that mean the opposite.

> The workers buffed the statue until it shone like a mirror.

Which word is a synonym for *buffed*?

> polished   covered
>
> tarnished   dismantled

Read the answers carefully. Which word means "to make something shine?" The answer is *polish*.

> When she feels morose, she watches funny cartoons to change her mood.

Which word is an antonym of *morose*?

> dismal   agreeable
>
> happy   confident

Think about the sentence. If something funny will change her mood, she must be sad. The answer is *happy*, the antonym of sad.

Analogies

This kind of question asks you to find relationships between pairs of words. Analogies usually use *is to* and *as*.

> **Green** is to **grass** as _____ is to **sky**.

Green is the color of grass. So the answer must be **blue**, the color of sky.

Roots

Roots are the building blocks of words. Many roots come from ancient languages, such as Latin and Greek. If you know what a root means, you can often guess the meaning of a word. Some words are built by adding prefixes and suffixes to a root. Some words are formed by joining more than one root. Note that the spelling of a root can change. Some roots can stand alone as English words.

Root	Language	Meaning	Examples
act, ag	Latin	do, drive	action, agile
ann	Latin	year	anniversary, annual
cardi	Latin	heart	cardiologist, cardiogram
civ	Latin	citizen	civilian, civility
cred	Latin	believe	credulous, incredible
dent	Latin	tooth	denture, dentist
fid	Latin	faith	fidelity, confide
fract	Latin	break	fraction, fracture
gen	Greek	born	genesis, regenerate
grat	Latin	pleasing	gratuity, grateful
hydr	Greek	water	hydrant, hydraulic
imag	Latin	likeness	image, imagination
ject	Latin	throw	inject, reject
lat	Latin	side	lateral, bilateral
leg	Latin	law	legal, legislate
lit, liter	Latin	letters	literature, literary
loc	Latin	place	local, location
log	Greek	word, study	logic, dialogue, biology
mar	Latin	sea	marine, maritime
mech	Greek	machine	mechanic, mechanism
migr	Latin	move	migrate, immigrant

Root	Language	Meaning	Examples
nov	Latin	new	renovate, novitiate
pater	Latin	father	paternity, patrimony
rupt	Latin	break	erupt, interrupt
sign	Latin	mark	signature, signal
son	Latin	sound	consonant, resonate
spec	Latin	look, see	spectator, expect
tempo	Latin	time	temporary, extemporize
terra	Latin	earth	territory, terrain
tox	Latin	poison	intoxicate, toxin
urb	Latin	city	urban, suburb
ven	Latin	come	convene, convention
voc	Latin	call	vocal, evocative

Prefixes

A prefix is one or more syllables added to the beginning of a word to change its meaning.

Prefix	Meaning	Examples
aero-	air	aerospace
extra-	beyond	extraordinary
hyper-	excessive	hypersensitive
il-, in-, ir	not	illegible, inactive, irregular
mega-	large	megavitamin
mono-	one	monoculture, monorail
multi-	many, much	multipurpose, multiword
nano-	one billionth	nanosecond
out-	surpassing	outbid, outdo
tele-	distant	teleconference
trans-	across, beyond	transact

Suffixes

A suffix is one or more syllables added to the end of a word to change its meaning or to change it do a different part of speech.

Verb Suffixes

Suffix	Meaning	Examples
-ate	make	necessitate
-en	cause to be	deepen
-ify	make	beautify
-ize	cause to be	legalize

Noun Suffixes

Suffix	Meaning	Examples
-ance, -ancy, -ence, -ion, -ity, -ment, -ness, -ship, -ity	a state of being	vigilance, infancy, turbulence, explanation, generosity, assignment, kindness, kinship, modesty
-ant, -ent, -er, -or, -ist	one who	attendant, resident, hitter, actor, chemist

Adjective Suffixes

Suffix	Meaning	Examples
-able, -ible	capable of being	enjoyable, divisible
-ful	characterized by	careful
-less	without	useless
-y	like	thirsty

Adverb Suffix

Suffix	Meaning	Examples
-ly	like, resembling	quickly

Roots, Prefixes, and Suffixes

1. How does a hyperactive child behave?

   doing a lot, being very active

2. His story sounded credible. How did it sound?

   like you could believe it

3. The woman went into cardiac arrest. What part of her body was affected?

   her heart

4. His speech sounded very mechanical. How did it sound?

   like a machine

5. Where would an extraterrestrial come from?

   beyond the earth

6. What is a toxic substance?

   a poison

7. What would you clean with a dentifrice?

   your teeth

8. Left turns are illegal at that corner. Why shouldn't you turn left there?

   It's against the law.

9. What do migratory animals do every year?

   move from place to place

10. Who is your paternal grandfather?

    your father's father

11. What do spectacles help you do?

    see

12. How long does it take for a tree to grow an annual ring?

    one year

13. What does an ape do when it vocalizes?

    calls

14. When you temporize, what are you trying to gain?

    time

15. What kind of waves does sonar use to detect underwater objects?

    sound waves

16. Where is a maritime province located?

    near the sea

17. Whose rights do civil laws protect?

    civilians

18. What kind of energy creates hydroelectricity?

    the energy of running water

19. What do you do when you gratify someone?

    please them

20. In what direction does a quarterback throw a lateral pass?

sideways

21. What does a literary critic write about?

literature

22. What does an interurban train run between?

cities

23. What does an infidel lack?

faith

24. What is a monologue?

words spoken by one person

25. What does a locator do?

find things

26. You put a pencil in a glass of water. How does refraction affect what you see?

The pencil looks bent or broken.

27. The ruptured pipe caused the basement to flood. What happened to the pipe?

It broke.

28. What is a characteristic of a multi-venue celebration?

It occurs in many different places.

29. What is the most remarkable thing about an innovation?

its newness

30. The superhero's car has an ejector seat. What does it do?

throws him or her out of the car

Word Cube

Categories: *Partners,*
Visual Learners

Work with a partner. You will each need
a sheet of paper, a pencil, tape, and a
pair of scissors. Each of you
chooses six of the current
chapter's vocabulary words
and makes a Word Cube.
To make a Word Cube,
draw six squares in a shape
like this on the paper.

Write in each square one of the
vocabulary words you chose. Then cut
along the outside lines. Fold and tape the
sides of the shape to make a cube. Take
turns rolling the cubes. To score a point,
write a sentence that makes sense, using
the two words that were rolled. The first
player to get five points wins the game.

Vocabulary Commercials

Categories: *Small Group,*
Technology

Work with two partners. You will need
several sheets of paper and a pencil. On
one sheet of paper, list the vocabulary
words from the current chapter. Then
make a list of things you use every
day—a bowl, cereal, shoes, and so on.
Choose one of the items you listed and
write a TV commercial to advertise that
product. Write a script that lets all three
partners play a role. Use at least 10 of the
vocabulary words from the current chapter
in your commercial. Practice acting out
your commercial. Share your commercial
with the class by making a video or by
presenting a skit.

Creating Categories

Category: *Small Group*

Find two partners. You will each need a
sheet of paper and a pencil. Each partner
writes three of the current chapter's
vocabulary words that are related in some
way. For example, you might list words
that are all used to describe people, that
are all nouns, or that all describe ways to
move from place to place. Challenge your
partners to guess the connection between
the words you listed.

Conducting Interviews

Categories: *Partners,*
Technology

Work with a partner. You will need a
sheet of paper and a pencil. One partner
will be a news reporter and interview the
other. The reporter writes questions to ask
in the interview. The questions should
contain at least 10 of the vocabulary
words from the current chapter. The
person being interviewed answers the
questions, using vocabulary words if
possible. When the interview is complete,
switch places and let the other partner
write questions and conduct an interview.
If possible, record your interview on audio
or video to share with the class.

Crack the Number Code

Categories: *Partners,*
ELL

With a partner, write 10 sentences using
the current chapter's vocabulary words.
Next, assign a number to each letter of
the alphabet (A=1, B=2, C=3, and so on).

Code all the words in your sentences with the numbers you have assigned. For example, the code for the sentence "The cat sat on a mat" would be the following:

20, 8, 5 + 3, 1, 20 + 19, 1, 20 + 15, 14 + 1 + 13, 1, 20

Once you have coded all the sentences, exchange papers with another group nd try to "crack the code." The first team to figure out all the sentences wins the game.

Crossword Puzzle

Categories: *Individual,*
Visual Learners

Prepare for the game by bringing to class crossword puzzles from newspapers or magazines. Use these examples as a guide to create a crossword puzzle using the current chapter's vocabulary words. The word clues for "across" and "down" will be the vocabulary word definitions. Use graph paper for the crossword grid.

When finished, exchange puzzles with a friend and complete it. Return the crossword puzzle to its owner to check for accuracy.

Vocabulary Board Games

Categories: *Partners,*
Visual Learners

Find a partner and discuss types of board games you like to play. Talk about the object of the game, the rules, and the equipment needed. Then create a Vocabulary Board Game. Think of a way to include the current chapter's vocabulary words in the game. For example, the vocabulary words could be written on word cards. When a player

lands on a certain square, he or she must draw a card and define the word.

Create a game board on an open manila folder. Find or make game pieces, and write a list of game rules. Exchange Vocabulary Board Games with classmates and play their games. Keep the board games in a designated spot in the classroom and adapt the vocabulary cards for each new chapter.

All About Alliteration

Category: *Small Group*

Alliteration is the repetition of initial sounds within a sentence. Work in groups of three or four to create alliterative sentences that contain the current chapter's vocabulary words. The only words that can be used that do not start with the initial letter are *and, in, of, the, a,* and *an.* The object of the game is to see which group can come up with the longest sentence. (It can be silly, but it must make sense.) For example, using the vocabulary word *timid:*

The tremendously timid tiger tossed twelve tasteless trees toward the terrified turtle.

Word Sorts

Categories: *Small Group,*
Visual Learners

Work with a partner. Divide a sheet of paper into four sections labeled *Nouns, Adjectives, Adverbs,* and *Verbs.* Write each of the current chapter's vocabulary words in the appropriate section. When you and your partner feel that you have successfully placed each word in the appropriate box, turn your activity sheet upside down. (Allow only three minutes to complete this step.)

When the time has elapsed, exchange activity sheets with another pair and check for accuracy. (Use your *Vocabulary in Action* book for clarification.) The pair of partners with the most correct answers wins the game.

For an additional challenge, change the part of speech of the vocabulary words by using prefixes and suffixes. For example, if the vocabulary word is *migration*, you could add the verb *migrate* and the adjective *migratory*.

Good News, Bad News

Categories: *Individual, Partner*

Write a good news and bad news letter to a friend or relative. Alternate sentences that begin "The good news is" with sentences that begin "The bad news is." Use one of the current chapter's vocabulary words in each "good news" sentence. Use an antonym of that vocabulary word in the "bad news" sentence. For example, if the word is *compliment,* you might write "The good news is I received a compliment from my teacher for doing a nice job on my research paper. The bad news is I gave my teacher an insult when I forgot to say "thank you.""

For an extra challenge, leave blank spaces for the antonyms and exchange papers with a friend to complete.

Proofread Pen Pals

Category: *Small Group*

Find a friend and work together to write a friendly letter that includes at least six of the current chapter's vocabulary words. Your letter can be about school, sports, friends, family, or any other interesting topic. (Use a resource book to help you with the correct form for a friendly letter.) Include errors in your letter, such as spelling, punctuation, capitalization, and word meaning.

When you have completed your letter, exchange it with another pair of partners. Correct the new letter. After all the corrections have been made, return the letter to the original owners. They will make sure all the errors have been found.

Vocabulary Dominoes

Categories: *Small Group, ELL*

Begin the game by writing all the current chapter's vocabulary words on index cards. Write the definitions of the words on other index cards.

Place all the index cards facedown in the center of the playing area. This will be the domino bank. Each player chooses four dominoes as his or her supply. Turn one domino faceup to begin play. The object of the game is to match the words with their definitions.

If Player 1 makes a match, he or she places the two cards down on the table, and Player 2 chooses. If Player 1 doesn't make a match, he or she must take a new domino from the bank. If that domino doesn't match either, the player must add it to his or her supply. Player 2 then tries to make a match. The first player to match all the dominoes in his or her supply is the winner.

Impromptu Stories

Category: *Small Group*

Write each of the current chapter's vocabulary word on an index card. Shuffle the cards and place them facedown in a deck. Players take turns drawing five cards from the deck. As each player draws cards, he or she makes up a story using the words on the five cards. Players can use any form of the word listed. To make the activity more challenging, try to make the players' stories build on one another.

Vocabulary Sayings

Category: *Small Group*

Find three partners. Write down the following five sayings:

Birds of a feather flock together.

A rolling stone gathers no moss.

Too many cooks spoil the broth.

A penny saved is a penny earned.

A stitch in time saves nine.

Then brainstorm other sayings. When your list is complete, rewrite the ending of each saying, using a vocabulary word from the current chapter. Example: Birds of a feather sit on our overhang.

Try to create two new endings for each saying. Share your list with other groups or create a class bulletin-board display of your work.

One-Sided Phone Conversations

Categories: *Small Group, Auditory Learners*

Find a partner. Work together to write one person's side of a phone conversation. Use at least 10 vocabulary words from the current chapter. Be sure to include both questions and answers in the conversation. When you have finished, find another pair of students with whom to work. Read your one-sided conversation to the other pair. After you read each sentence or question, ask them to fill in what the person on the other side of the conversation might have said. Then listen to the other pair's conversation and do the same. Try to use vocabulary words as you create the second side of the phone conversation.

Mystery Word Web

Categories: *Small Group, Visual Learners*

Find three partners. Draw a word web on a sheet of paper or on the board. One partner chooses a vocabulary word from the current chapter and fills in the outer circles of the web with clues about the word. The other partners try to guess which word is being suggested. Each partner should take at least two turns describing a word. Be sure to include the Challenge Words in the activity.

Vocabulary Answer and Question

Category: *Large Group*

Gather these materials: poster board, 20 index cards, a list of the current chapter's vocabulary words and definitions, tape. Tape the tops of the index cards to the poster board so that they form five columns of four cards. Under each index card, write a vocabulary word. Divide into two teams and line up in two rows facing each other. Flip a coin to see which team goes first.

The first player chooses and removes an index card, revealing the word beneath it. The team has 20 seconds to provide the definition of the word in question form. For example, if the word *usurp* is revealed, a correct response would be "What is 'to seize power from an individual or a group'?" If a correct definition is given, the team scores a point and the next player in line takes a turn. If an incorrect definition is given, play passes to the other team. The first person in line chooses a new index card. Play continues until all the cards have been removed. The team that gives the greater number of correct definitions wins.

Dictionary Dash

Category: *Small Group*

Find three partners and divide into two teams. You will need a dictionary, a sheet of paper, and a pencil. Write 10 vocabulary words on index cards and place them facedown on the floor. The first team turns over a card to reveal one of the vocabulary words. Each team should then look up the word in the dictionary and record the following

information about the vocabulary word on a sheet of paper:

how many different definitions the word has

the correct pronunciation

the guide words located on the dictionary page

a sentence that uses the word correctly

When both teams have finished, exchange papers and check for accuracy. The team that finishes first and has no mistakes receives two points. If the other team makes no mistakes, it receives one point. The game continues until all vocabulary index cards have been turned over. The team with the most points wins the game.

Vocabulary Haiku

Category: *Individual*

The word *haiku* comes from two Japanese words that mean "play" and "poem." A haiku is a poem that contains 17 syllables. It is written in a three-line format. The first line has five syllables, the second has seven syllables, and the third has five syllables. Frequently, a haiku describes a scene in nature.

Using the current chapter's vocabulary words, create your own haiku. For example, here is a haiku for the vocabulary word *harmonize*:

Soft falling raindrops
Harmonize with the children
Playing in the rain.

When the class has created several haiku, collect them and create a book. You may also wish to read your poems aloud to the class.

Word Wizards

Category: *Small Group*

Find three partners and divide into two teams. Choose one of the current chapter's vocabulary words. Each pair of partners writes the word at the top of a sheet of paper. The object of the game is to write as many forms of the word as possible by adding prefixes, suffixes, and word endings. For example, using the word *scribe,* you could write these words: *scriber, scribing, script, prescribe, subscription, subscribed, scribed, subscriber, subscript, subscribes, subscribe, subscribing.*

Each round should last three minutes. At the completion of a round, teams exchange papers and check for accuracy. Use a dictionary to clarify any questions.

For each correct word form, one point is awarded. For example, the above list would receive 12 points. Use a new vocabulary word for each round. The team with the most points at the end wins.

Captions

Categories: *Small Group, Visual Learners*

Find two partners. You will need old newspapers or magazines, scissors, paper, and glue or tape. Clip five pictures from the newspapers or magazines. Write a caption for each picture that describes what is being shown. Include at least one vocabulary word from the current chapter in each caption. Attach the captions to the photos and display them in the room.

Vocabulary Charades

Categories: *Small Group, Kinesthetic Learners*

Find three partners. Write on a slip of paper each vocabulary word from the current chapter. Fold the slips and drop them into a box. Partners take turns selecting words and acting them out. The actor may not make any sounds. The first person to guess the word earns a point.

Password

Category: *Small Group*

Find three partners and divide into two pairs. Write on a slip of paper each vocabulary word from a chapter. Divide the slips evenly between the teams. One partner will be the "giver" and the other the "receiver." The giver views the word on the first slip and gives the receiver a one-word clue about it. The receiver tries to guess the word. If he or she is correct, the giver goes to the next slip of paper. If the receiver is wrong, the giver gives another one-word clue. If the receiver does not guess the word after three clues, the giver goes to the next word. The team has three minutes to cover as many words as possible. A point is awarded for each correct answer. The second team then has three minutes to go through its words.

Pledges

Categories: *Partners, Visual Learners*

Work with a partner. Think of ways to improve your school or community. Write a pledge that lists the things you will do to make improvements. Use vocabulary words from the current chapter. Make an illustrated bulletin board of class pledges.

Step Up Vocabulary

Categories: *Large Group,*
Kinesthetic Learners

Have the class form a line along one side of the room. Designate a "goal line" about 15 feet away. Ask players in turn appropriate questions about the current chapter's vocabulary words. For example:

What is the definition of (the vocabulary word)?

Use (the vocabulary word) correctly in a sentence.

What is a synonym for (the vocabulary word)?

What is an antonym for (the vocabulary word)?

What is the root word of (the vocabulary word)?

Name three forms of (the vocabulary word)?

What is the present/past/future tense of (the vocabulary word)?

If the player correctly answers a question, he or she may advance one step toward the goal line. The first player to reach the goal line is the winner.

Word Volleyball

Category: *Large Group*

Divide the class into two teams and have them line up facing each other. Toss a coin to see which team goes first. Say one of the current chapter's vocabulary words. The first person on Team 1 must provide a synonym for the word. Then, like in the game of volleyball, the word is sent back to Team 2. The first person on that team must provide another synonym for the word.

Play continues until one team cannot provide a correct synonym. The team that provides the last correct synonym scores a point. Say a new word and continue with the next player. This game can also be played using antonyms.

Class Debate

Categories: *Small Group,*
Technology

Divide the class into an even number of teams of four or five debaters. Give pairs of teams the pro or con side of issues they may feel strongly about. For example:

TV has nothing good to offer.

Students should wear school uniforms.

Everyone should learn a foreign language.

Allow 10 minutes for teams to prepare their arguments. Each team must use at least three of the current chapter's vocabulary words in its presentation. Have the teams present their arguments to the class. Have the class choose the winner of each debate. You might make a video of the debates so the students can see themselves.

Listen to This

Categories: *Individual,*
Auditory Learners,
ELL,
Technology

Some English-language learners may be more proficient in oral than in written English. Record each of the current chapter's vocabulary words followed by a slight pause and then its definition. Let individuals listen to the complete recording several times. Then have them listen to each word, stop the recorder, and define the word themselves. They can then listen to the definition to make sure they were correct.

Same and Opposite

Category: *Small Group*

Use this activity for reinforcement or reteaching. Write on index cards each of the current chapter's vocabulary words.

Write a synonym and an antonym for each word on separate cards. Shuffle the synonym and antonym cards and place them facedown on a table. Distribute the vocabulary word cards evenly among a small group of students. One student turns over the first card in the pile. Players must look at their vocabulary words to see if that card is a synonym or antonym of the word on the first card. If it is, he or she takes the card and places it faceup on the table with its matching vocabulary card. Continue until all the cards have been matched. The player with the most matched sets of three wins.

What's the Word?

Category: *Large Group*

Write each of the current chapter's vocabulary words on an index card or self-stick note and display them on a bulletin board. Tell the students to try to use the words during the day. When a student uses a word in an appropriate way, he or she gets to take the card. See who has the most cards at the end of the day.

Here is a list of all the words defined in this book. The number following each word indicates the page on which the word is defined. The Challenge Words are listed in *italics*. The Word Study words are listed in **bold**.

Index of Words   Level H